A Holi of Poetry

(An Anthology of Odia Poems in English Translation from Seven Odia Poets)

A Holi of Poetry

(An Anthology of Odia Poems in English Translation from Seven Odia Poets)

Arupananda Panigrahi
Bijayketan Patnaik
Haraprasad Das
Hrushikesh Mallick
Kamalakanta Panda (Kalpanta)
Prabhanjan K. Mishra
Runu Mohanty

Edited & Translated by
Prabhanjan K. Mishra

BLACK EAGLE BOOKS
Dublin, USA | Bhubaneswar, India

Black Eagle Books
USA address:
7464 Wisdom Lane
Dublin, OH 43016

India address:
E/312, Trident Galaxy, Kalinga Nagar,
Bhubaneswar-751003, Odisha, India

E-mail: info@blackeaglebooks.org
Website: www.blackeaglebooks.org

First International Edition Published by
Black Eagle Books, 2023

A HOLI OF POETRY
by **Arupananda Panigrahi, Bijayketan Patnaik, Haraprasad Das, Hrushikesh Mallick, Kamalakanta Panda (Kalpanta), Prabhanjan K. Mishra & Runu Mohanty**

Edited & Translated by **Prabhanjan K. Mishra**

Original Odia copyright © Individual authors
Translation copyright © Prabhanjan K. Mishra

All rights reserved. No part of this publication may be reproduced, stored in a retrieval system, or transmitted, in any form or by any means, electronic, mechanical, photocopying, recording or otherwise without the prior permission of the publisher.

Cover & Interior Design: Ezy's Publication

ISBN- 978-1-64560-427-3 (Paperback)
Library of Congress Control Number: 2023943630

Printed in the United States of America

Dedicated to

Jayanta Mahapatra
Eminent poet

Prabhanjan K. Mishra, the former president of Poetry Circle of Mumbai, former editor of this poet association's literary journal 'Poiesis', an award-winning poet, writes in a supple style both in Odia and English, using metaphors, symbols, motifs, mainly of Indian origin. His poems are replete with mild satire and irony. He writes generally on interpersonal relationship, landscapes, and social dichotomy. His literary politics leans towards the dregs of the society, the dispossessed mass. He is a poet, translator, critic, essayist and editor. Poetry is his first creative love. He has three books of poems to his credit and his poems and translations have appeared in more than twenty anthologies, Indian and overseas'. Widely published in journals. Has read his works in Poetry Festivals and from reputed platforms.

CONTENTS

Foreword, Introduction and
Acknowledgement / Prabhanjan K. Mishra - 11

ARUPANANDA PANIGRAHI

The Harvest – 17
For a Grain of Paddy (1) – 19
For a Grain of Paddy (2) – 21
Water March – 24
The Winter Night – 26
The Home is Like a Tree – 28
Twelve O' Clock, Midnight – 29
The Story of the Rocks – 30
Mr. Mysterious – 32
The Illusive Flowers – 33
The Pain – 35
The Bosom – 35
The Dung-beetle – 36
Two Maverick Wayfarers – 38

BIJAYKETAN PATNAIK

In Memoriam: Father – 40
The Terrorized Tusker-king - 42
Grieving in Three Dimensions - 44
The Overflow – 46
Don't Abort Me, Ma', Let Me Be Born - 48
The Busy-bee Man - 50
Tear in the Eyes of his Highness - 51
The Mountain Pass - 54
The Breath of Life - 55
Secret Celebrations with the Self - 57
The Touch - 58
The Wooden God - 58
Hunger - 60
The Sea at Chandipur - 61

HARAPRASAD DAS

The Marriage Night - 31
Remorseful Arjuna -65
Kadamba's Longing - 67
Hunting in the Dark - 68
Animal Sacrifice - 69
Jesus Christ - 71
The Forgiveness - 72
The Jasmines - 73
Dvapara - 74
The Body - 76
Ultramarine Kohl - 77
Self-immolation - 78
God in the Mountain Pass - 82
Deification - 83

HRUSHIKESH MALLICK

Tumbles Down Your Coiffed Hair - 85
The Goat-herd Girl - 91
Dak Bungalow - 95
How Could the Sea Breach the Trust - 98
Home, Sweet Home - 101
Autumn - 102
I am from 'Mao-Cadre' (I)   105
I am from 'Mao-Cadre' (II)   108
Taila's Concept of His Homeland – 109
An Elegy to My Ruined Crop - 111
For You, Imraanaa, Only for You - 112
My Big Brother's Wife, Utterly Motherly - 115
The Struggle - 119
How Did You Celebrate your New Year Day? - 121
Karna - 123
If One Promises the Moon to His Wife - 125

KAMALAKANTA PANDA

The Song of Silence - 127
Wish You Well, Sweetheart - 128
The Tree - 130
The Distances, No More Distant - 131
The Rains - 132
Jagannatha, the Lord of Puri - 135
Monsoon - 136
Solitude - 137
Cyclone and The Timid Village - 138
Corona - 140
A Roll call for Saora - 141
You - 144
The Cyclone, Mango Tree, and
the Poet Jayanta Mohapatra - 145

PRABHANJAN K. MISHRA

Father: Nostalgia - 148
Heart: A Window - 150
Snapshots from Dusk - 152
Purposeless - 153
U-Turn - 155
Pushing a Hurtling Cart, the Time - 156
Night Vigil -158
Commitment - 159
Grey Sorrow: Salty Tears - 160
Aging Mona Lisa - 162
Skin-deep Fame - 163

RUNU MOHANTY

The Painting Studio - 165
The Whore - 167
The Woman - 169
Ektara - 170
The Adoration - 172
The Prayer - 173
Manali - 175
The Flight - 176
The Divine Union - 178
Fair-weather - 180
A Sufi Song - 181
The Story of a Moonlit Night - 183
The dance is Over - 185
The Boarder, Upstairs - 186
Only for your Sublime Presence - 187

Foreword, Introduction and Acknowledgement

A HOLI OF POETRY. Holi is the festival of colors for Indians. It is celebrated by smearing or splashing colors on one's dear ones, transforming the everyday world into a brilliantly-hued, vibrant one. Here are seven poets of the Odia literary world, writing and celebrating as if with colors of the Rainbow that the readers would find highly enjoyable and evocable. These poets are of a highly evolved class, having practiced the sacred art form of poetry with admirable and unique styles. Their poems are no doubt a platter spanning, in general, the landscape of Odia poetry, offering its sublime *rasa*s (aesthetics and tastes) and *bhava*s (expression).

Only seven Odia poets were considered for this volume for various limiting factors. The first and foremost reason is the constraint of space that the publishers impose. The second and the most important one is they write very contemporary genres, shifted from the conventional styles, representing an inner world of Odia mind.

With my dealing with poetry for about four decades of reading, writing, critiquing, translating and editing, I find it difficult to place a poet in the spectra of poetic-scape in respect of his or her style, consistency, reflections, and intent, unless I have read several poems of the poet spanning over years of his writing. Even ten poems of a poet written in various periods of his life may feel hardly adequate to judge the poet. So minimum ten poems of each poet have been collected in this anthology to give an overall feel of the poet's creative quality and nature to the readers.

If more poets were to be considered, the number of poems had to be reduced per poet at the cost of giving the lovers of poetry a real feel about the poets. I have come across many anthologies of Odia poems and quite a few of translated works and have personally faced similar hardship. I have arrived at judging a poet's potential wrongly by reading one or two poems included in an anthology that I have repented later when I followed the poet's work with a larger prospective.

The seven poets in this collected work reflect different moods and reflections of Odia life. Like in the festive Holi of Colors, the seven poets bring home several vivid expressions and hues of moods. They craft their poems in their unique formats and genre, and with unquestionable honesty. Like a flock of peacocks, they present the vibrant plumages of Odia literature - the native adages, idioms and dictions prevalent in Odia social life in their poetry. It has been a pleasure to read these poets, and to translate their works. I would like to give a brief glimpse of my understanding of each of these poets and their poems.

Arupananda Panigrahi is rooted deeply in his native soil. A poet from the house of old-time village farmers, he dreams of mud, lichen, bullocks and the paddy grains, even while sitting in the cloistered confines of his chamber as a senior Banker, crowded with cash, cashiers, customers, and crisp currency notes streaming out of ATMs and counting machines. A queer combination of the material world and poetic moods. His main fortress of creativity is built on farming, harvesting, and pastoral life. Societal elements constellate in his mind in the middle of worldly humdrum. He speaks in metaphors collected from rural tranquility and urbanized turbulences. A marvel of combination of mind, matter, and machine. He blends mud and musing. His poems interweave joy and pathos.

Bijay Ketan Patnaik started writing poems of love and yearning from an early age that got published in Odia literary magazines. Later, he fell in love with the flora and fauna, especially of the wild variety, of jungles, hills, estuaries, marshes and other natural retreats away from human settlements. His poems, like his essays and travelogues about virgin nature being defiled, reflect his primal love for the mother earth. Also, his poems reflect his relationship with his native soil, parents, and family. His poems have a touch of leaning towards the unaffected raw-innocence. Often, he writes with a tongue-in-cheek, giving his poetry a punch of salt-and-pepper. He can be very sarcastic about the powers that be, even about God and the archetypal bhakti.

Haraprasad Das is one of the benchmark-writers/poets/critics of Odia literature, and one of the living greats of poetry-craft, with dexterity in poetic expression and philosophy in Odia as well as in English. He writes in an imagist and cryptic articulation. His dense imagery and exactness of delivery presents a challenge to translating his works, at least what I faced during working on his poems. I often felt inadequate in bringing alive his sense and style, his multilayered voice. His works dwell over outdated societal practices, like animal sacrifice and blind devotion, and reflect the attitude of a reformer. He used satire and irony as tools to deliver his intended targets. His works seem to defy the time with an all-time-relevance. His poetry has been applauded with awards and appreciation.

Hrushikesh Mallick is a much-experienced professor of literature, teaching Odia language, but to me more of a natural poet, poetry being his food, drink and thought. He seems a lover of quaint Odia culture connecting him to his nativity and nostalgia. His famous work 'Jeje Dekhinathiba Bharat' (roughly translated - 'The India, Grandpa Missed'), is a soft satire of modern tinpot developments that try to erase our fond heirlooms of the sober and honest culture. He liberally dips his pen into the ink of Indian myths, like his exposition, say, on Karna, the controversial hero of Mahabharata, besides looking at things ruefully through the eyes of his late grandpa. He writes in a style with dark humor, critical of the new tinpot version of the progress. He cries for the rights of the poor and the dispossessed of the land. He has been decorated with many laurels and accolades for his lifelong contribution to Odia literature as a poet and critic.

Kamalakanta Panda has the distinction of perhaps being the most-known, published and the most-read and appreciated among the Odia poets over half a century, yet not having a single book of his poems from any press. His philosophy is that he would write as a lover of poetry, very privately like undressing and changing into a fresh set of clothing by a papal officer in his cloistered sacristy, but in the process would never expose his vulnerable underbelly. He bothers little if his expositions are going to create a ripple, a protest, a titter, or an ovation. Once he was tied and beaten in public by miscreants for exposing a sex-racket in his poems, but he remained undaunted. It would surprise the readers to know that he has not been awarded even once, because the award-committees never work 'suo moto' to recognize the worth of the artists; they are rather helpless within their framework to go ahead without recommendations of earlier reputed voices. He writes excellent poetry and in recent times, is using quaint

Odia words from the past, a unique experiment to enrich the Odia language by bringing alive these forgotten and comatose but musical and metaphoric words to give a new voice to the poetry.

    I have also taken a few of my own Odia poems for my translation and placed them in this Holi of Poetry. In my own judgement, I find myself using an urban tongue peculiar to my spending the majority period of my literary life in cities. My poems reflect interpersonal relationship, the social dichotomy, and double standards in the society, often leading to self-doubts creeping into my poetry, making them multi-layered. I have often reflected on landscapes in Odisha and outside that I have come across; I have discovered in them a communicating persona with a voice peculiar to each of them. If I read my poems like a reader detached from my own creative self, they read metaphorical and cerebral. I mostly use Indian myths, legends, symbols and motifs. Satire, irony, transferred epithets are my poetic tools besides other poetic devices and accessories.

    Runu Mohanty, the only female voice in this cluster of male-presence, stands distinct by her writing on feminine angst. Her poems are spiritual as well as sensual in the same breath, befuddling a reader if she is addressing them to her lover or to God, a feeling similar I get while reading Tagore's Gitanjali. She can stand neck to neck in her Odia poetry to the famous Indo-English poet Kamala Das from Kerala, having the edge and capacity to make her poems have an honesty and dignity about female sexuality. Her poems are dominated by a woman's anxiety regarding her dignity against the prevalent gender-bias. Her poetic female persona speaks fearlessly in a society that thinks like a male in most matters. To me, in battles of gender-oriented poetic combat this poet finishes with the last word and the last laugh.

During editing the body of my translated work that has been going on for the last three years, I have tried to make them read and sound like poems written in English originally by the poets themselves. The poets in this collected work have obliged me to select and translate their poems and I feel grateful to them for appreciating the final product. I acknowledge with bowed head their trust reposed in me.

I am **grateful to the eminent poet Jayanta Mohapatra** for finding time to look into the manuscript of the anthology and enrich it with his valuable suggestions, besides appreciating certain areas with his comments as a poet. I take the liberty, on behalf of all the poets here, for **thanking Dr. Mrutyunjay Sarangi** who published most of these translated works in his well-edited and popular **literary e-journal 'Literary Vibes'**. I also **thank the editorial staff of Kavya Bharati**, the Madurai based highly acclaimed literary journal, to have published quite a few of the translations included here. I **am thankful to the poet Geetha Nair, retired professor of English literature**, All Saints College, Trivandrum, Kerala, to have contributed to the improvement of certain crucial poems included in the book. She has also expressed her personal satisfaction about poetry placed in the book. I **gratefully acknowledge the encouragement and ideas of Dr. Bhagaban Jayasingh**, Professor Emeritus, ASBM University, Bhubaneswar and his kind words. The last but not the least, **my heartfelt thanks go to the publishers Black Eagle and their motivator Satya Pattanaik** without whose cooperation, this effort would not have found an international platform.

- Prabhanjan K. Mishra.
(Editor, Translator)

Arupananda Panigrahi

Arupananda Panigrahi *is a senior Odia poet, his poems mostly rooted in Odisha's native soil; has four collections to his credit; he writes his poems in a spoken tradition in an idiom unique to his poetry. Sprinkled with mild irony, his poems subtly closet at their cores the message of hope even at the moment of proverbial last straw of despair. (email id – arupanadi.panigrahi@gmail.com)*

The Harvest
(*Amala*)

The season of harvest rules the roost -
caring two hoots for the loafing spring.
Paddy sheaves taste the vigor
of the threshers' log, after moving from

under the cattle hooves of *bengalaa**;
leftover grains get removed. A serene sun
peeps out, the air vibrates with bhakti songs,
coming all the ether-way from Cuttack Akashvani*.

A grain of paddy, a loner, a dreamer –
sky being its dream's limit, left out
in its sheaf, escaping the trampling hooves,
escaping the thresher's log;

away from joining his peers
in the ring of food-chain,
away from ending in a cooking pot;
along with dreams of endless possibilities -

Could be the primal seed, God bless,
the sole sire to a paddy generation of thinkers;
or the humble leaf curled up in its womb
containing a potent green revolution?

What, if the village boys
ask for a bundle or two
of the scrapped sheaves to build
the holy fire for Agira*, the fire-festival?

And the loner grain is fire-roasted
along with its sheaf, puffed out, dream and all,
and falls to a roadside walk, unnoticed,
getting crushed under an unwitting foot?

What, if the boys knead a strand of the sheaf
containing the dreamer into the mud
that goes to build the Devi Saraswati?
Lo! The grain is worshipped as the Devi's flesh!

What, if the Devi is immersed along with the grain,
the mud gets washed off by submerging water,
the dreamer coasting to the water-edge?
Would it lie, rot and die deep in the mud?

What, if it germinates, grows and dies alone,
as an unsung visionary of a paddy generation?
What, if it starts a colony of luxuriant crop
starting a new crop-age! A green revolution!

(*Bengalaa** - A method of removing grain from paddy sheaves, by putting them under the feet of a group of bullocks that keeps going in tandem round and round a central hub, trampling the sheaves underfoot. Akashvani* - Radio Station. Agira* Festival – A fire-rite, celebrated on the evening of Magha Purnima by the agrarian community of Odisha to usher in prosperity in the form of a bumper harvest.)

For a Grain of Paddy - 1
(*Gote Dhaana Paain - 1*)

The path to the north
from our house
led to the weighing station,
to the rice mill.

The one to south
led to our farming fields,
that sustained us; also,
to the cremation ground.

Father took paddy
to the weighing station,
to the rice mill
for weighing, de-husking.

But the day
eerie drone of cicadas
bothered us, as well the children's
sense of foreboding,

father had left the house
with his basket of paddy
by the backdoor, going south;

it made us apprehensive.
Would he reach
the field for showing,
or end up
at the cremation ground?

Golden paddy grains
would get scattered in fields,
seasonal sowing for the crops,
from father's iron-fist.

That would bring us
our morsels of food,
life's foremost joy
for a farmer family.

Each grain of paddy contained
the microcosm of a dream,
ours, we, the farmland dreamers,
we, the farmhand children.

The dreams reposed in reality,
in morsels of steaming rice.
Even mother never neglected
a single grain of paddy,

even a grain that fell off from a sheaf
offered to the goddess Lakshmi in our shrine.
Mother would collect it fondly in her
sari corner with other cast away grains.

A single grain of paddy
she would pick up and keep
from the last measure of paddy
sold to a merchant, symbolic.

She would save such grains carefully
as her precious tokens.
Each of these grains, perhaps she knew,
stored in its womb

a farmhand's
invaluable dreams,
his future, his past;
a measure of his present.

For a Grain of Paddy -2
(Gote Dhan Paain - 2)

My father, by his sorcery,
would sow fistfuls of paddy,
reap granary-full of grains.

A sorceress by her own standards,
my mother would convert quintals
of paddy into kilograms of fine rice

using her de-husking manual machine
the *dhenki* installed behind the house,
the heavy wooden pounding device.

My wife, another astute conjuror, would put
handfuls of fine rice into a boiling pot,
taking out a pot-full of steamed rice.

She would usher me into her parlor
to have a rice-meal by ten in the morning,
I, a punctual salaried employee.

I would have my daily fare
of steamed rice
as my breakfast-cum-lunch

by that time in the morning, before
going to office. I am no conjurer,
only a humble officegoer.

Ha! I would point out
to a paddy grain,
unhusked but semi-cooked,

sitting on top of the pristine rice heap;
like the Biblical mote,
in a neighbor's eye, a blemish.

The unhusked, uncooked
single paddy grain would bother all,
a spoiler of the fun of each conjurer's hard work!

Could it be the paddy grain
that my father had left out
from his carefully collected

small stock of seeding grains

for the next season of sowing?
Had it escaped my mother

and her pounding machine,
her attention wavered
at the de-husking *dhenki*?

Did my wife ignored it
while cooking the rice
in her rice-cooker?

Or did the cooker that had bubbled over
teasing my wife for her pockmarks on face,
making her absent-minded by its tease?

Father blamed my mother,
the mother blamed my wife,
but the wife found none down the line.

So, she put the tongue
firmly in her cheek,
and hissed at me with her harshest,

"What's the big deal, man? Hush!
Just pick it up and put it aside, down,
why make a fuss ?"

Water-March
(*Paani Paain Padayaatraa*)

Birds drop down from a parching sky,
the breasts of women droop dry,
the unwashed hairs hang loose, limp
from the heads of thirsty children.

The old man fails to urinate,
his entrails desiccated dry.
The shooter Ghinuaa can't wet his throat
before entering the jungle with a gun,
finds no game at the dry waterholes;
returns with a load of firewood instead.

Our MP visits Delhi to ask for water-wagons,
but returns as the minister of steel and mines.
The thatches with tinder-dry rafters
on our mud-houses look skyward for rain-clouds,
but are derided by the sun's firework.
We have everything, but not a pail of water.

Many a mirage dance before eyes, many delusions -
the cool wind brings tidings of a distant wetness,
the sun cracks the earth with fissures
and down the cracks, lurks a hope for water;
in late nights the grass feels wet
under-foot, we are confused, dew or rain?

How far would go this march, this search?
Do green pastures lie beyond horizons?
Why do then the thirsty birds come flying
to drop dead at our doorsteps?

Our fertile fields go fallow,
long for the past's water-abundance,
the cattle recall bathing in muddy abandon.
The traitor sun transports our moisture
to the poles, to pile up
as snow on their ice caps.

My friend, don't waste time in propitiating gods,
rather dig the soil, water might be waiting there.
Don't desist from digging, my people,
if your spade and crowbars hit buried articles -
sickles, snuff-boxes, or kohl-containers,
even toys; don't fight over their ownership;

you might have found a buried past,
not water. Don't digress if your quest for water
results in finding a holy lingam.
Digging for water, may bring serendipity,
turning you into a profound excavator!
Geological dark-horses may surface.

Snoring remains of an extinct civilization,
its buried ornaments, weapons, artifacts
lying beneath layers of the earth's soil.
You may discover many lost civilization
that thrived by riverbanks, going extinct
when the water courses died,
when droughts desiccated the soil.

Also don't get carried away by a gold mine,
stay on your target, dig for water.
You may dig so deep, when you look upward
the opening at the top shrinks

to the size a distant star. It may turn
impenetrably dark down there.

You may lose all your digging tools,
your orientation, but keep 'tooth and nail' intent.
You may die and get buried
in a waterless arid grave,
your thirst overpowering you
join a pervading silent dark, peace.

Get out of such traps, crap ideas,
try with consistency, brace yourself
for an ultimate sacrifice; the oblivion
that may wipe-clean your failure
even to yourself, your wrap wet with
your own blood, giving a sense of water.

The Winter Night
(Shita Raati)

In a small town,
a winter night
dwarfs all other seasons.

You hire a rickshaw
knowing well the fare is unfairly high,
but its driver is your bonus, a relief
when you take lonely roads in cold nights.

You bargain with him over the fare,
a routine practice in small towns;

blackmailing him, "If I go jogging home,
I would save the fare, reaching home warm."

"Why should I oblige the winter night
by hiring this rickshaw? Is it to entertain the silence
with the rickshaw's rattle; or just for the fun
of haggling over the unjust fare?"

But there lies another catch,
your camaraderie with the rickshaw-driver,
it gives you a friend to gossip with
on the tidbits of your busy day,
a time-pass mechanism - over bidis
and a shared lighter.

Would others ever know
the secret pleasure of this trip
in a cold lonely night?
For them the winter night,
the rickshaw, and the haggling
over the fare, the parts of life.

What would they know of the camaraderie,
the shared smoke over small talk,
the joy of a journey with a temporary friend
in a lonely cold winter night?

The Home is Like a Tree
(*Bruksha*)

When our house caught fire,
the inferno charred my innards
inflicting unseen wounds and hurt.

People from the close by market
joined my pa, grandpa,
in dousing the fire;

it seemed - our ancestors from
the ashes in the cremation ground
came bounding to give a hand.

My grandpa, the bravest of all,
entered the holocaust, untethered
the cattle, took them to safety.

Father, nervous and apprehensive,
by disposition, salvaged
our land revenue documents.

In spite of my youth and daring, I failed
to do much; only could unhinge
the front door, carrying it away to safety.

The fire put out, the sundry firefighters
gone home; we, the homeless lot,
were inconsolable like orphans.

I remonstrated, "Grandpa,
how helpless we stand,
our home reduced to ashes!"

Grandpa consoled, "My son, a home
is like a tree, half above the ground
and half inside the earth.

"The visible half of our home
lies in ashes, but the half where we really live
lies safely ensconced in our hearts."

His words of comfort spurred us.
Lo and behold! We built a lovely hut
by the next morning, a home feeling so homely.

Twelve O' Clock, Midnight (*Raati Baa'ra*)

In my lexicon, the real nightfall
happens at midnight,
roads go deserted,
though a few drunk drivers
ride home late from pubs.

It's time for fishermen
to go out to the sea to spread their nets;
but I, a sedentary man, sit
by my table by the window, sleepless,
with a pen I am in love with.

My eyes ajar, I gloss over
a pair of pigeons
dozing on my window sill,
their inky dark shapes skim the night
for patterns of words for my pen's tip.

If a nightly squall comes by,
it would pass by like a thief,
barely leaving marks,
as does the silly graffiti by children
on the smooth bark of our guava trees.

Let labourers snore
in their restful slumber.
Allow me, the classic idler,
too lazy even to have
his forty winks,

spend his insomniac nights
in star-gazing or counting waves.
Don't engage me in chores
like counting eggs before they hatch,
or pumpkins before fruition, too laborious.

Rather ask me to do what I am good at -
watching the night sail by
at the open window by my writing desk,
and marveling at the pink new sun
bringing blush to guava cheeks.

The Story of the Rocks (*Paashaana*)

The river sighs to her parched bed,
the stream having stopped rippling
and murmuring to the reeds.

Isn't it time dear, we
stop romancing on its banks,
stop throwing stones into its dry bed.

Shouldn't we go down to listen
what do the rocks, small and big,
lying huddled on the dry riverbed

have to say? So far, not a word
of squabble or one rubbing another
the wrong way has been heard.

Perhaps, the lack of water has muffled them.
See, their rocking and rolling in the current
has rubbed them off their rocky features –

they lie around like frozen teardrops,
but without dripping, as it is said,
'A rolling stone gathers no moss'.

How do these smooth featureless rocks
pass time on a dry bed; sitting
cheek by jowl without a word?

My sweetheart, let's select a big rock
to sit on, spread our legs to put on a smaller one,
and listen to the silent rock-music;

rejoice as they do, sprawling about,
the little pebbles and big stones,
reminding us of our rocky future.

How would it feel, if I etch
your name during our love's paroxysm
with my chisel onto your rocks?

Would it spark a fire, bring us our
propitiate time, and illuminate
the blind rocky alleys of our future?

Mr. Mysterious
(*Parichaya*)

Shouldn't you be more friendly
with the crocodile in a river
if you live by that riverbank?

Wouldn't it sound rude asking
the visitor his name, address and purpose
as soon as he comes along?

Of course, caution is your hallmark,
a householder, you can't trust
a stranger in your neighborhood.

You may soften your inquiries like –
"Are you passing by this area, brother,
to some other place? Another destination?"

A neighbor may whisper
in your ear, "Take care man,
the stranger could be a robber."

"He may walk away stealthily
with the women's clothes drying outdoors
that save your household dignity."

"Imagine women without their clothes!
Wouldn't their honor be questioned
and gossiped like that of *Gopi*s of *Dvapara*?"

A well-wisher may caution,
"The fellow could be an imposter,
may steal cattle from your shed."

But by the next morning,
you find him gone; leaving harmless
footmarks and rubbing on the wet sand;

looking like the blurred smears
of a slithering big reptile
as it drags itself into the river.

The harmless stranger is gone, he still
unknown despite telltale marks left behind.
You accuse yourself to have suspected him.

The Illusive Flowrs
(*Michha Phula*)

"Don't pluck flowers. You are allowed
only to play around the bushes."
The children feel let down
with the gardener's tough warning.

What would they play with,
if no flowers be plucked for their playhouses?
The flowers would wither away
in a few hours. Isn't that a sheer waste?

The children have a doubt. Are these flowers
real or artificial ones stuck to the bushes?"
They obey the gardener, but
not before taking a closer look.

At home they find
beautiful flowers swinging
in a calendar, looking lovelier
than the ones in the garden.

Even a few dewdrops
appeared to linger on the petals.
They caressed them, touched
them with fingers and lips.

The flowers in the calendar
felt alive and real: they
communicated with the children's
inquisitive mind, their playfulness.

They concluded: the flowers
in the garden were unreal, rather stuck
to the bushes for the visitors' watching.
Plucking would betray the secret.

Unreal as the characters
in story books. Even people on streets
may not be real people. Oh, they can shout,
but loudspeakers shout too.

The Pain
(*Kashta*)

I am blind,
so is my flute;
it's toneless as well.

I attach my mouth
to its lips,
fingers to its eyes.

It starts singing,
my lips go mute,
pleasureless.

The Bosom
(*Chhaati*)

The sun is going down,
long shadows
measure the ground,
the last sun is still on the terrace.

Some gossips flap wings.
But neighbouring terraces
behaving like strangers, gossips there
practise the art of silence.

Your sari doesn't show your loveliness
to advantage, spread it for airing
in the terrace sun. its crispness
may bring your shape alive.

You look elegant in saris
of lighter shades,
your contours stand out
in white saris.

The night's darkness subsumes
a wind that plays like a petrel with
your sari's wraps, playing black and white.
Even jackals of the night go berserk.

The Dung-Beetle
(*Gobara Poka*)

(1)

Behind our house by the dung-pit
mother would make dung-cakes
by flattening and drying
rounded dung-lumps, her cooking fuel.

The dung rolling in her hands
would be sweet music to our ears;
would churn stomachs
with the hope of a hot meal.

Our childish hands itch
to join her home-industry,
get trained by her by the dung-pit,
often spoiling her hard labour.

But it would be a rite of passage,
redolent of love, her and ours,

from the dung-pit to kitchen,
from fuel to hot fresh food.

Like the mother bird in her nest
feeding titbit to her babies,
putting food into their tiny mouths;
so, they grow, fly and forage.

We, the children, eat, grow and take off;
but do we worry, what keeps
our mother alive? The mother-bird
picks and survives on dung-beetles!

(2)

The squelching sound of dung
in mother's kneading hands
would make our mouths water,
churn bellies for a hot meal.

Every piece of dung cake,
burning in the kitchen stove,
would bear her finger marks,
aglow in a lovely ember-red;

as well, would glow there
her silver finger-ring, once lost
and buried in the dung-pit, now embedded
in a piece of dung-cake, luminous in the woven;

a relic of her love
and legacy, her sacrifices;
but the finger that wore it,
that is now beyond the mortal touch.

Two Mavericks
(*Baatoi*)

I feel like having
a word with my father.
Even I am not sure,
what would we talk about.

Daily, we come face to face
many times over, pass each other,
without a word, as if,
having nothing to say.

He looks at me, expectation in eyes;
as do my eyes brimming with questions,
nothing comes to my mind;
does he also feel tongue-tied?

When I come before him,
often my mouth goes dry,
the tongue loses its way,
and spit chokes my throat.

Perhaps, father knows me
better, his shy son. His eyes,
twinkling with affection, hover over me
when I pretend to be in sleep.

Father is approaching me,
may I have a word with him?
None seems to be around
to make me feel shy, tongue-tied.

Perhaps, we both go about
like strangers, our worlds
being separated, as well as joined
by a cold bridge crying for warmth.

I search for that inviolable bridge
to join our worlds of hesitation,
inhibition, inward struggle; having
walked long parallel, tiring distances.

The bridge yet awaits our footfall,
its edges florally decorated
for our welcome, but gathers dust,
crying for the dust of our maverick feet.

Bijayketan Patnaik

Bijayketan Patnaik is a sensitive word crafter, agile with poetic diction and nuances. He weaves an uncanny world out of the social issues, human feelings, and awakes the spirits of his readers like a motivational leader. He is widely published in Odia, including his four collected works. He has carved a space a space of his own in the contemporary literary scene of Odisha. By profession, he has worked as an officer of the Government of India at very high levels in the forest department, and his intimacy and attraction to the flora and fauna often gets reflected in his poems.

In Memoriam: Father (*Baapaa*)

Father's sweat and blood
oozed into little rivulets;
he tilled our drought-dry land.

He raised crops,
taming discordant songs
from the green nubile shoots
till they ripen to brown paddy.

The difference from mine,
he tuned his poetry while
etching the lines with a plough.

The irregular lines
written as poetry by riff-raffs
paled before his soulful furrows.
In childhood, my little feet
were unable to walk
long distances.

I rode his shoulders
to village fairs at Gurujang
and Dhableshwar.

I recall those rides,
much more comfortable
than cars and scooters today.

In cool moonlit nights
in our inner courtyard,
father lying on his back,
would make me a *gugupaanchi**.

I would watch the moon play
with the floating clouds while
swaying on that knee-swing.

The *Baali Jaatraa**
where he took me
to ride the giant wheels.

When the evenings loomed
over the cow-dust in village lanes,
father would sing devotional songs.

The plaintive sweetness would
fill our souls - 'How long would you,
my Lord, keep me waiting...?' I never
would know for what did he kept waiting.
I would rejoice in his Bhakti songs
while busy in my homework,
the light melody, a booster
to arithmetic and sociology.

As tranquil as my mother's lullabies,
better than melody nights
of today's DJs. His evening song-soirees
made us mini-monks out of spoilt brats.

(*Gugupanchi** - adults, lying on their backs, would swing little kids on their bent knees. *Bali Jatra** - rural fairs held on dry and sandy river banks and seashores of Odisha, the fairs starting with the day of Kartik Purnima, to commemorate the seafaring trade and traders or *Sadhav*s of ancient Odisha, using *Boita*s, the large country-crafts.)

The Terrorized Tusker-King
(*Aatankita Gajaraaja*)

In the past I ruled these jungles;
my writ ran under my royal title,
the "*Gajaraaj*", Tusker-King.

I roamed the jungles, my kingdom,
with my entourage, the royal court
and my queens and children.

My kingdom, the jungle, is going
to ruins; delicious bamboo shoots
and succulent foliage dwindling,
waterholes drying away by alien onslaught.
Our free movement is hampered
by boarded up elephant reserves.

Trains run along tracks splitting
our ancient elephant-walks,
the iron leviathan at times,
cutting us to pieces;

if we retreat,
death-traps await behind,
dug-up trenches to catch us
for zoos, circus, or cheap transport.

We fall prey to greedy hunters,
their bullets; to poachers, their poison;
wires carrying high-voltage block our escape;
we stay cooped up in house arrest.

I, the *Gajaraaj*, the tusker-king,
feel trapped in this hell-hole,
our so-called safe haven,
the government elephant reserve.

I, the impotent king, too helpless
to save my subjects as its patriarch head.
The good word 'progress' sounds like
a curse to my ears, in my usurped land,

crisscrossed by rail-tracks, canals,
and roads; my jungles deforested
for setting up factories, its labor-camps,
or to build houses for the landless settlers.
Hungry, thirsty, in search of food, water
we stray into human habitations,
but we are driven ruthlessly
back into our enclosed reserve to die

without food, water and our quiet shelters.
We are chased with fire, stones and sticks,
beating of drums and deafening fire-crackers.
We run tucking our tells, terrorized.

Grieving in Three Dimensions
(Shokara Tinoti Pankti)

When My Youngest Daughter Died
Your arrival was fortuitous,
neither desired, nor intended;
yet, you came bringing us
a spring in our lives' winter-days.

An unexpected of happy sequel,
that but ended unceremoniously.
"Good things don't last, *que sera sera*."
our mutual consolation bleeds!

When My Eldest Son Died
You always seemed to me
as my just-born baby, out of my womb
after nine-month-gestation.

Even in death, you seem
to be there, as a spark of my soul,
a chip of my block, a habit of my habits.

Your throbbing memory
would keep you alive in me,
but what of your new bride?

She shared your life just a night,
her night of consummation
spent in your bed, the first ever with a man.

Would that give her a memory
to last the lifetime? Or too inadequate
to long for you, to yearn for you?

When My Husband Died
I recall, our birth-charts
being matched by astrologers
for good luck and hefty nuptials
before getting bonded together.
The priest blessed, "Live endearingly
in this everlasting togetherness."
My father emptied his purse,
for celebrations matching
the priest's predictions, but
you left unannounced.

What a travesty! What a hoax!
Our nest lies in tatters.
A bond is broken.
Long live the bond!

The Overflow
(*Oottaran*)

Let rice water
boil over, spill.

Boiling milk on the stove
overflows, the sea in hightide
breach the shores,
the history outwits myths.

The societal progress surpasses
the fatalistic folks, blind believers.

The pride and arrogance
spill over and
flow out, the ego bursts
like the bubbles in a froth.

Follow suit the delusions,
also, the pomposity and prejudices.

One is but a lone pilgrim,
a poor, plain sentient being,
peel off his masks, affectations,
his real persona is a vulnerable aspen leaf.

Everyone sails in a rudderless boat;
is adrift in a desolate sea,
awaiting moksha,
awaiting his last release.

Words overflow with feelings
to make poetry,
the day outgrows its limit
to die in the arms of a night.

Rivers in spate overflow banks,
the sea overflows
into the land in a tsunami.

If a good-for-nothing fellow
is overreaching his limits,
let him.
What would he possibly achieve?

Castles in the air?
The fools' paradise?

But ask an Olympian archer,
what would he do if he missed the target,
His humble reply may be,
he would try again.

If I had to move away
before the Champak,
I planted, flowered, shouldn't I
bear with the hazards of living?

Transfers come
with a government job;
so, we move. One day,
I have to leave this world too.

Have to leave my dear ones,
like a lone pilgrim leaving home

to walk to a pilgrimage,
I would leave body for the unknown.

We squeeze our wet laundry,
and wet napkins, for excess water
to outflow, excess sweat wiped off

our foreheads.

I have been squeezing myself
the whole of my life,
a doubt bothering me,
what would flow out in the last squeeze?

Blood? Tears?
Or would there be
the fruits of my lifelong labor
burnished golden?

Don't Abort Me Ma, Let Me Be Born (*Dharavataran*)

Give birth to me, ma;
from your dark womb.
My eyes long to see
a serene day, feel quiet nights,
your radiant beauty.
Let me rejoice in them.

Deliver me,
the flesh of your flesh,
let my first cry be
the echo of a new life
amid the silence
of aborted female embryos.

Let me, your little girl,
grow into a woman,
the green shoots spread
into a tree, flower your dreams;
roots going far and wide:
your myths, history, heritage.

Let me lie in your arms,
drink at your breasts,
learn the A, B, C of life
at your feet. Your wisdom
etched on my clean slate.
A woman's esoteric mystique.

Train me be a nation-builder,
a doctor, an engineer, a scientist,
a poet, a woman of substance
with the finest intellect and instinct,
a wife, a mother, a homemaker,
or an architect of the destiny of people.

Give me the support
of your finger, ma, to cross
my toddler days, guide me through
difficult adolescence;

channelize my bubbling youth
into a pastoral serenity.

Let me take birth, let me see
the light of the living world,
do not abort me ma,
your female fetus, your girl child.
Do not nip me in the bud,
let me come, let me be, ma.

The Busy-Bee Man
(*Byasta Loka*)

Selfishness breeds
escapists, opportunists;
who keep stealthy watch on others,
filling their honeycombs by robbing others.
It makes wolves wear the looks of lambs,
all along fooling the trusting *Red Riding Hood*s.

There goes a man, busy as a bee,
made of different clay;
he works with the poor laborers
crushing his bones,
mixing blood with sweat and tears,
earning his crumbs.

He raises his flag of protest
in the vanguard of every protest,
be it of farmers, of laborers,
who ask for freedom from penury,
freedom from oppression;
in dhoti-*gamchha** on his lean body.

With a scythe in hand,
he chops off symbolically
the harvest of dark forces,
chops off the weeds,
sifts the poison seeds
sown by the exploiters.

He relishes and cherishes
the breath of the wet earth,
delights with the green shoots
rippling across the barren fields.
He welcomes a bright tomorrow
by waving high his torch of free thoughts.

He dreams of the power that be
vested in the hands of common man.
I, a humble poet, would cherish and write
the manifesto of this busy-bee-man,
build his myth out of an aura,
an age, a belief, a mountain of light.

(*Gamchha** - a napkin used to cover the upper part of the body and also to use as a towel. A wrap of a common man in Odisha, Bihar, UP and Assam.)

Tear in the Eyes of his Highness
(*Chhamunka Aakhi Luha*)

Why do the royal eyes well up?
By God! Something is amiss,
terribly wrong! Are the people
of the kingdom on the run?

Have his ministers deserted him?
As well the courtiers, servants,
Queens and attendants?

Why are his royal cheeks
wet? Has anyone
been critical of him, of his whims?
Who did the daring?

No dearth of flowers
in the royal gardens,
the rivers are feeding
the royal lake perennially, keeping
its water sweet and abundant.

His excellency runs his writ
over the powers over his fiefdom,
the arbiter of its destiny.
His mandate is the gospel truth.

His fragile tolerance
can't be labelled as intolerance,
his hunger for wealth is no greed.
His instant decisions are not whims.

In addition to behaving
mute and deaf,
his wishes and whims
make the land's mandate and law,
create conventions.
His bravado is bravery.

He is the monarch
of all he surveys,
he is God, the preserver,
terminator and deliverer
of his mute subjects.

His writ runs absolute.
Even time holds itself still
at his command
before deciding its motion
from past to the present, to future.

Why is his excellency weeping,
shedding invaluable pearly drops?
Is it a feeling of loss, missing
a goalpost, or being stung
by the barbs of conscience?

Has his royal existence
been questioned
by the turned-coats?

In neck-deep in opulence,
is he missing the taste
of ordinary savories
from the hurtling cart
of his childhood street peddler?

And, what of the court-jesters
who are to keep his majesty in splits?
Or have they been ordered to allow
him the luxury of crying?

"If I cry, I will shed pearls",
was his handmaiden myth,
but his tears defy his own mandates.
Have the flatterers fled, afraid of the truth?
Tears from the royal eyes
instead of pearls!

Something is terribly amiss,
what has gone wrong, why do
the exalted cheeks look wet?
Where are his men, his courtiers,
and soothsayers who would
forecast 'all is well',
subscribe to his infallibility?

The Mountain Pass
(*Ghaati Raastaa*)

The life's hill-pass snakes ahead
as does a hair clip snuggling
into the bunched-up hair of a woman.
The hill-path hugs rock-leviathans,
uncoiling along thin vipers,
or crossing the pythons of rivers.

Precarious journeys produce believers,
the travelers remember their gods, though
the gods hardly shoulder the responsibility,
rather reminds the man of hollow homilies.
The poet sings, "*The paths of glory
lead but to the grave*". Ha!

Life trudges along, a long winding
mountain pass in the vehicle of flesh.
Born of the elements, it would
return to the elements,
as does a ripe palm fruit
flops down to the ground.

The life's mountain-pass
may be lush, lusty and alluring,
rising inexorably but the past returns
a haze on the horizon – a toddler walking
along the childhood's nursery,
the kindergarten, school, and college.
But one day, all stand transfixed,
undecided, if to move ahead or retreat?

Footnote - *The quote is from poet Thomas Grey's poem "Elegy Written in a Country Churchyard". The stanza goes like:
"The boast of heraldry, the pomp of power,
And all that beauty, all that wealth e'er gave,
Awaits alike th' inevitable hour,
The paths of glory lead but to the grave."

The Breath Of Life (*Sworodaya*)

You are a dream merchant sir,
trading in dreams in exchange of the reality.
Promises - Wealth, lucrative job, big house,
a stable of cars and a bevy of servants;
almost a kingship in blink of an eye.

A poor daily wager,
I earn a pittance. My hunger
is fed with single nightly meals.
I don't daydream,
as well spared by nightmares.
Thank you.

With bargaining art, par excellence,
an astute trader encrypted into your DNA,
you offer castles in the air
in exchange of our real fish and salt,
ivory palaces for our water and earth.

Born poor in humble ensembles
of thatch and mud, reinforced
with wooden rafters, our great gods
sitting in little alcoves; here: we light
our prayer lamps, light our pyres.

If our forefathers come down to rejoice
a night under a serene moon
of their native land, they may but get
the shock of their life. Your tinsel town
would give then silent sobs, long sighs.

Until I am dead, until my native heart
has stopped beating,
let me delight in my nativity,
rejoice in the scent of my soil.
Hey Ram, bless, let my land stay with me.

The Secret Celebration With Self
(*Ekaa Ekaa Utsav*)

This celebration is all mine,
I alone hold all its cards without brouhaha,
play it like a game of solitaire.

I am the sole host, also the sole guest,
the usher, the attendant,
and the priest of this ceremony.

None is expected anyway;
all, fair-weather opportunists,
who pull vanishing acts in hard times.

This occasion, a celebration
of my loss, my ruin, like the last rites,
a pity, of a wounded underbelly I hide.

The holy month of Muharram
to a grieving Maulana, a winter fire
to a jungle, a spot of blood of puberty.

Had the friends and relatives come,
would have made me the butt of their jokes
over goblets of wine at my expense!

This is my festive dark, my wounded pride,
my insular sacristy where I hang
my blood and tear-soaked wears.

I feel cloistered and sheltered here
within the four walls of my anguish,
with myself, my wounds, my secrets.

The Touch (*Sparsh*)

My intents eager to touch you,
but you recede away, a moody lotus,
the pond is slippery,
you seem ever out of my reach.

Unsure of taking my pick
from among your lips, chin, nape or navel,
or the pool down the steps?
What does my explorer zeal seek?

A live volcano in sleep,
a melting icy glacier in wait,
any of them would devour me
if I take a plunge.

Peeling layers of silk and satin,
digging into the soft dough,
could there be a surprise in wait?
A scaffolding of bare bones!

The Wooden God (*Darubramha*)

Holding myself still and unmoved
seems beyond me. Underfoot,
the ground gives away, quicksand.
The plaster and paint get peeled off
from time's ramparts, I feel unstable
both in space and time.

Wish, I had the ability

to keep my feet firmly on the ground,
navigate the world's length and breadth,
like the *'Vaman'*, with telescopic limbs,
taking control of all I see,
doing that in no time.

Is it necessary to be mobile?
Should it bother anyone if I stay still?
If I can hold my ground,
let the earth underfoot slip away.
Let my wooden avatar, without moving a finger,
go places riding an wooden accelerator,

even move into the lush grass
in lawns drenched with morning dew.
Wish I had robotic arms,
in spite of my immobile stance,
to caress the green leaves on trees,
comb the feathery puffs of cotton-clouds

swimming across the sky. How I wish,
my wooden avatar could reach out
to pluck the *Parijat** from Eden, dig out
the *Baidurya Mani** from the earth's womb,
fill the world with *Parijat*'s fragrance,
dispel the dark with *Baidurya Mani*'s brilliance.

(Footnote – *Parijata** is a flower of heavenly beauty and fragrance. *Baidurya Mani** is a gem of unparalleled luminance and good omen.)

Hunger
(*Bhoka*)

If a hungry mother
feeds her embryo with rancor,
a terrorist would be born.

The child born hungry
would stay hungry and
cry sucking the dry tits.

Hunger turns the soft
rounded bosoms into
harsh shriveled pouches.

Unkind, ungiving, unyielding.
The little one grows feeding
on hunger, anger, biting empty bowls.

He kicks open the doors early.
His path opens to a road
leading to the dark wilds,

where the terror breeds,
hatches as violent dinosaur eggs
on hungry stomachs.

More lethal than bombs,
more sudden than land mines,
more trigger-happy than gun-runners.

The hunger teaches
to pick rice grain
from the garbage-bins.

Hunger wins new territory,
as he grows,
from stomach to flesh.

As an avenger, he loots for food,
the rich hoarders; he rapes to feed his flesh
the fashion divas, at the receiving end.

Black-marketeers,
socio-political tormentors,
haughty socialites fear him.

His hunger, a devouring fire,
captures him, an insect in a spider web,
more he struggles, he grows hungrier.

His incessant fight to survive,
to breathe, drink, eat, turn him
into a cruel criminal.

The Sea At Chandipur
(Chandipur Ra Samudra)

Why were you angry?
You didn't allow me
to have an eyeful of you;
you ran away
beyond my eyes' reach.

I remonstrated, begged you
to stay back, but you paid two hoots.
You looked away moody, whimsical,

putting aside my entreaties,
you walked back to distant oceans.

Wished, you had looked back and
noticed little kids in multihued clothes
walk behind you, coaxing you
back to safety of the shore
from drowning in the deep ocean's pits.

You said, you would return as in the past,
but you forgot to take back the shells
you had scattered on the sands.
Your crabs feel unsafe out of water,
they scurry helplessly into holes.

Local women are walking around
in your sand with baskets on hips
to pick dreams, the lovely sea-shells,
that you left behind for them,
to sell to tourists to buy frugal meals.

At a distance, Balaram Garhi basks,
the fishing port with power-boats
and fishing-trawlers awaiting your return
to go with you into the deep sea
for filling the sails with the wind of hope.

Your sulk is fickler than the ice cream
that melts if taken out of the refrigerator.
It has its own mood and time to decide
how much, how far and when.
An unpredictable spoilt brat.

Haraprasad Das

***Haraprasad Das** is one of the greatest poets in Odia literature. He is also essayist and columniat. He has twelve works of poetry, four of prose, three translations and one piece of fiction to his credit. He writes in a cryptic and metaphoric genre using satire, dark humour and irony as his tools. He is bilingual in writing and his creations in English carry equal dexterity as a poet and critic. He is a recipient of Kalinga Literary Award (2017), Moortidevi Award (2013), Gangadhar Meher Award (2008), Sarala Award (2008), and Kendra Sahitya Akademi Award (1999).*

The Marriage Night (*Madhushajyaa*)

The auspicious fish-amulet
blazes on bridegroom's turban
to usher in good luck
to the solemn union;

and the motif
of golden pitchers,
brightly embossed
on the bride's sari.

The sari-hem covering
the bride's pretty head
slips down, and her confidence;
she flounders in a limbo,

looking for an identity, declared
as 'married', having shed the baby-fur
and the baby-fat; swimming out of
the pubescent sea, she wonders, *"Who am I?"*

She sprawls, weighed under
her bridal splendor, on an opulent bed,
beneath the canopy of a translucent net,
a fig leaf to hide the open-secret.

She resents the impromptu hand
groping her guarded spaces,
caressing her undone hair,
touching her softest privacies.

She wonders, "Is this man
looking for a site
to hoist his flag, a page to put
his stamped signature of ownership?"

But would the man ever find his wife
on that bed - between the sheets,
beneath the net, in her undone hairs,
in her secret spaces?

Possibly, before he finds
the right site for his flag or the page
to put his signature, she would be gone
to an unknown address.

Nothing, neither the solemn rites,
nor the sacred amulets, fish or pitcher,

could put the two impromptu strangers
together to steer the marital ship.

The bed would wait in vain
for fulfilling its much-lauded purpose,
giving the man his ownership,
the wife, her identity!

The nuptial bed would lie disconsolate,
feeling like made of bare bones
with sheets of thorns,
the net hiding secrets of a failed bond.

Remorseful Arjuna
(*Abasadara Rathare Jane Arjuna*)

With tears in eyes,
Arjuna remorsefully
hurtled ahead in his chariot.
He failed to comprehend
the bloodthirsty war-flags
fluttering atop his cousins' war-tents.

He knew, the killer instinct killed,
arrows and swords
were only excuses,
as was blood, labeled as instigator.
His arrows agreed with him,
they hesitated to leave his bow.

The arrows, perhaps, couldn't
differentiate foes from the family,
both bleeding the same red blood,
hurting equally, but anointing
the winner as the prince of absurd,
wearing the crown of unease,

sitting on the throne of vainglory,
soaked with family-blood.
Arjuna took an eyeful of the battle field
from the prospective of an open eye
of a slain soldier lying on the ground,
staring out of its macabre socket -

Neither the dumb sword,
nor the unfeeling arrows
suffered from guilt,
but in the guilty soil of the war field
and repentance stroke deep roots;
excuses never redeemed the killings.

He commiserates with his wife,
"O' exalted princess of Drupada,
do not ask me for your bloody retribution
as the price for our love.
It would break your slim hip with too heavy
a pitcher of blood, carrying it to posterity."

Kadamba's Longing
(*Keli Kadamba*)

The lore of Dvapara
may be fading into sepia,

the folk-memory
going blurred over the millennia.

Years sailing by waving 'bye'
to the newly arrived ones,

but a solitary Kadamba by Yamuna
hopes against hope, "Krishna would come.

"I would celebrate my spring-blossoms
in Krishna's company;

"get my longings fulfilled
by my Krishna's loving fingers

"moving through my tousled hair, the foliage,
stoking my skin, the scabby barks

"from drinking the stone's sap.
The time would hold breath in celebration."

The Kadamba is
getting bald, her foliage no more

supple young, her virgin sap drying
weighed down by her dreary years.

Hunting in the Dark
(*Mrugayaa*)

Why should a woman feel grateful
if her rich and powerful paramour,
takes her to bed, but spares her
from being an unwed mother?

Jungle-justice of the hoary past
still prevails in today's society.
Dushyants, today's social-lords, defile
Shakuntalas, the jungle-nymphs.

A vacant lot in Kharabela Nagar*,
of late, has painfully witnessed
a gang of rowdy Dushyants
ravaging a hapless Shakuntala.

The honor of women
remains unsafe in hands
of their macho husbands
balloons of boastful machismo,

also unsafe in the hands
of leaders who keep repeating
hollow homilies like stale vegetables
heaped at market's garbage dumps;

equally unsecure in hands of the police
who chase away the vultures
swooping over the victims,
allowing them to return, finish the job.

Ours, a land of incompetent pretenders,
wielding power but behind smug masks,
fore-planning to let Shakuntals be ravaged,
let miscreant Dushyants go scot-free.
Footnote - *Karabela Nagar – a dense residential area of
the city of Bhubaneswar.

Animal Sacrifice
(Upaaya)

Don't be appalled
by the dripping blood.
This is your share of meat,
the *prasad* from the sacrificial altar.

Take it home,
cook and eat with family and friends,
enjoy the mood of festivity
in social company.

A bit gruesome, but nonetheless,
it is a delightful ritual.
See, the oozing blood
doesn't make me uncomfortable.

Of course, it may return
as a nightmare, scary.
I may even scream
like a *Gangashiuli**

finding blood on its pristine
delicate white petals.
But isn't that
a different matter?

Why should you mind?
So much one gain, losing so little.
Great social gains for so small a price,
costing us only our innocence.

Oh priest,
anoint us with
vermilion, garland us.
Let's dance

to the frenzied drumbeats
like possessed devils,
with abandon
to the macabre rhythms.

Let this opiate seduce us,
oiling our social engine,
steamrolling merrily
over our innocence.

(*Gangashiuli* – the small delicate fragrant night-jasmine with white petals on a little orange stack, also called '*Ratrani*', the night-queen.)

Jesus Christ
(*Yishukhrista*)

Where are you, little one?
I sense your footfalls
in the wind's rustle
across our bereft courtyard.

Be happy, my child,
wherever you are.
Let my conscience,
that moved heaven and earth

to recover from you the cost
of my few drops of blood,
carry the burden of that cross
a while more, penance for my blunder.

I dream of the day
I may pass the litmus test
to stand neck to neck
with your moral benchmark.

You would be the chosen one, I know,
for the Lord's Holy Shroud,
even if the history would lay the Lord
differently in His immortal coffin.

The Forgiveness
(*Kshamaa*)

Making excuses, asking forgiveness,
keep increasing –

A guilty boat
lies listless in a repentant river.

Stars wear sorry faces
accused of being inauspiciously aligned.

The repentant night joins in procession
with the penitent sun.

The pontificating self-pride
follows suit for contrite lame excuses.

Walking on the footsteps
of an unforgiving world,

the right kind of words may save
the situation for me, help me dodge

ever-increasing supplicants.
But using the words to my advantage

may not save my soul from the guilt
of inability to forgive them all.

I fear, it may convert me
into a cruel wordsmith

carving beastly sweet-sounding babel
of a savage.

The Jasmines
(*Malli Maala*)

O' queen of my heart,
place these jasmines
at the Blue Lord's feet;
the fragrance, left
in your palms, would be
enough for holding me in a thrall.

Before leaving
for my lonesome dwelling,
let me wish you well, and
to all your admirers, gathered here
on your dance floor
to steal an hour or two of joy.

My house in my absence
would be lying orphaned and helpless,
its floor could be flooded from open taps,
clean laundry stacked on the floor
soaked, soggy, swimming. The thought
gives me goose-bumps of fear.

Unwashed dishes in the sink
would whet my hunger,
the grubby cockroaches
on kitchen wall will be walking

in circles around the old aerial rod,
the Ursa Major around the Polestar.

The aerial rod obstructing
my angry roach-swatter,
delaying their *moksha*,
journey to their roach-heaven
from the misery
of their pest-life in my kitchen.

These are the grim realities
of life, o' the queen bee of my hive,
of the splendid dance-floor,
that fills us with joy for a few hours,
the cameo amid life's drudgery,
and sending us home with smiles in pockets.

I would also take dreams home,
to infuse my household with it.
They would turn into jasmines,
suffusing my home, stealing
from you a garden of sweetness,
the fragrance from your hands.

Dvapara

If you have no knowledge
of how the divine couple
spent their night
by Yamuna in their lush arbor,

their bower lit by a star's glow,
an excuse for light.
If you are not privy to the lust
that dragged them

by hand to the amorous
land of ecstasy,
then, steel your heart
to hear the truth.

It's nothing less or more
than the ubiquitous game
played in the secret garden
of flesh, in the name of divine.

Neither a wrap was spared,
nor a fig leaf; not the unabated
flow of sweat and spit,
until they won the promised land.

The flying of sacred flags
atop the holy shrines,
is a ploy for the blind believers,
much ado about nothing.

It is rather the wounded time
hanging on the crucifix of a suspect saga.
Its arrow, having hit a wrong target,
lying blunted, thrashing in pain.

The Body
(*Deha*)

Go ahead, touch it,
it's tangible, it is sentient;

a pretty paradox
from the birth to dust;

an enigma
enough to chew for a lifetime.

Hack it to pieces
to your heart's content;

burn it with lust's tinder
all your prime.

To satiate the dead forefathers
offer it as *Pinda*, tire it with penance;

the ritual rice-ball offered
on a platter of banana leaf,

a leaf withering in hot sun's fire,
a fig-leaf for penance.

Consign it to water
to float away to the other world;

consign it to fire
to rise as smoke to heaven;

consign it to earth's humus
to salvage the soul to eternity.

Your body,
your slave,

a wishful star,
caught in desire's sooty cobwebs,

sleepwalking with you
until the last curtain.

Ultramarine Kohl
(*Nilaanjana*)

To come off my high horse,
courage was not enough,
rather, pretenses came handy.

When floating among clouds,
my image, resplendent
by the glow of the day,

fell into the water
scooped in your palms
to be offered to the sun;

and you fell in love with me.
I was not there
to share your tears of joy.

Believe me, in spite of
my best efforts, I could not come down
below my station to be with you.

Changes however
crept in surreptitiously
like the Bay of Bengal

changing colors quietly -
the meaning of love and pride
changing in my lexicon likewise.

Of late, I feel like being
your inseparable shadow,
unable to stay apart.

Wish, I smeared my timid love
by your eye-shores as ultramarine kohl,
color of the deep-blue sky.

Self-Immolation
(*Atmadaana*)

It hardly matters
who remains loyal
to whom, and how long;

who bothers to say 'bye',
to whom before leaving; but
the bald *Jaamun* branch

bangs its head as reminder
against the half-ajar door
at every departure.

It is not clear
who has gone halfhearted
to the ruined sylvan land,

and who before returning
has serenaded the silent ruins
with a few quatrains

from the melody of a grand
musical symphony,
might it be tonelessly.

No one is really worried about
who died hanging,
after making a joyous home

with love and sacrifices,
but choosing the noose to be
the best choice for an honorable exit.

The past is to be erased
and one is to march ahead
to the goal, still far ahead -

the innocence
of sinless lichen to be extracted
from the fish stomach;

the unsavory virtues
to be delivered
even by tortoise-transport;

the values of life to be salvaged
by the skin of teeth
before they sink to abyss;

sense to be put into bland prayers,
fallow land to be tilled
to sow seeds of hope;

if needed, engaging
in gory violence to get even
with an unforgiving past.

One is to keep in mind
that the need is desperate
to press ahead,

changing strategy,
wearing various guises,
beating obstacles,

negotiating pits and bumps,
falling and rising again and again.
Believe me, one is to forget

small and big lapses,
panting ahead in mad haste,
burying underfoot

the memories,
even if a sweet past
is erased unwittingly.

Great distances
are yet to be negotiated,
the goal remaining out of bounds;

the whirlwind uncomfortably closer,
already churning at the street corner
may reach the doorsteps any time;

one has to face it
even if the limbs are weak
and incomplete;

even if the mud walls are raw,
too soft to fend
against the onslaught;

even if as weak as an improvised
mud throne for the king
instead of one of solid gold.

The ultimate oblation
might have been poured
into the sacrificial fire,

but the resplendent flames
are yet to rise
from its smouldering bed.

God in the Mountain-Pass
(*Ghaatire Ishwara*)

Rambling discussions
through the night
made us lose
the count of time.

Meanwhile, an unknown hand
had unsheathed a morning
like a shining knife
out of the hill's waistband.

Yesterday, an unknown hand
had hurled a string of pearls,
in the shape of a constellation of stars,
over our village mustard field?

Our bus was now negotiating
a precarious riverbend.
Once again, uncannily
the selfsame hand

from its hideout,
staying out of sight,
helped us cross safely
the perilous mountain-pass!

Deification
(*Avataar*)

No one has free time to go–
one is taking pumpkins
to Hari-Raajpur market
on bicycle to sell;

another is busy
shooting birds
embossed on
the linoleum floorcovering.

After finishing studies,
climbing to the top
of my career graph,
taking all the dips in *Vaitarini**,

I have retired and is rather free;
like the sliver of light
that has entered a *pukhraj**
flashing back and forth

from the inner lattice faces
unable to come out
of the gemstone, the ray
trapped in a gemstone prison.

Thus deified, I am trapped
by my own achievements,
abilities, successes and sacrifices.
I have to but go –

Stumbling along the mud road
bruising my ivory elbows,
soiling my brass feet, to catch the last bus
that might blind me by blowing dust into eyes.

(Footnote – *Vaitarani**, the river, symbolizes *moksha* after purification from sins by taking a dip in its holy water and crossing to its other sinless bank. *Pukhraj** is a gemstone like diamond that imprisons light inside its lattice faces emitting a sparkle when a little of the light escapes.)

Hrushikesh Mallick

Hrushikesh Mallick – *The poet has been solidly entrenched in Odia literature as a language teacher in various colleges and universities, and as a prolific poet and writer with ten books of poems, two books of child-literature, two collections of short stories, five volumes of collected works of his literary essays and critical expositions; besides he has edited an anthology of poems written by post-eighties' Odia poets of the last century, has translated the iconic Gitanjali of Rabindranath Tagore into Odia; and often keeps writing literary columns in various reputed Odia dailies. He has been honoured with a bevy of literary awards including Odisha Sahitya Akademi Award, 1988; Jhankar Bishuv Award for Poetry, 2011; Sachi Routray Poetry Award, 2016; Sharala Puraskar, 2016; Bhanuji Rao Memorial Poetry Award, 2018; and Cental Sahitya Akademi Award, 2021. He writes in a commanding rustic voice, mildly critical, sharply ironic that suits his reflections on the underdogs and the dregs of the society.*

Tumbles Down Your Coiffed Hair (*Phitigalaa Tama Sajadaa Gabhaa*)

(Part - I)
The poet is out,
on the lawn; it's late night,
wife by his side,
his inseparable shadow.

Muted yellow marigolds
grieve for the dying moon,
waft a tragic sweetness
oddly reminiscent of flowers

offered at a dear-departed's casket.
The wind is sad and listless,
the lawn's eyes look welled up, the dew,
the poet's senses lurch into a gloom.

To lift the lid off the pensive mood,
his hands go fickle,
plucks a marigold from a bush
for wife's lovely coiffed tresses.

The gloom lifts, her hand cosy in his,
they walk with joyous abandon
on the lawn, exuded by
marigolds of a romantic mood,

awash with cool drops of dew,
dimly reflecting the snoozing moon,
languidly hanging on horizon,
a muted Chinese Lantern.

The wife's feet get wet with dew,
its wetness wash away unwittingly
the pink *Alataa** smeared there
like a blush to her nubile feet.

Upset, she glares at the lawn, glares
at the dew, glares at her husband,

her withering frown roasts them all -
the lawn, the dew, the poor poet.

But with unsuppressed mischief in eyes
the poet tucks the marigold in wife's hair
Butt her coiffed hair tumbles down,
not less than a *second sin**;

hundreds of uncoiling black asps,
a waterfall flowing down into the night
inviting the poet to get wet,
and regale himself in its cascade.

But her face clouds, the poet
ignores her anger as mock,
her love's complicity intriguing him,
a weaver bird's complex weaving.

Their mutual quadratics, braiding
a sun with a no moon, the poet
revelling in its double nooks and creases,
her caprice of moods, childlike gaiety.

The poet feels puzzled – why does a lily
wither in its water-world when the rest
of the flower-sisterhood hails the rising sun?
Why do deciduous trees of a jungle

shed leaves and stand naked in shivering winter?
Why do eyes go moist with tears
in night's most soulful hours of union?
Ah, a travesty, or a poetic irony!

At his wit's end, the poet cajoles
his sweetheart to listen
to the night's muted musical notes,
the murmurs ranging from tenor to soprano -

the distant bullfrogs and cicadas in bushes.
He begs her to forgive the dew
that washed her *Alata**, and the marigold,
that undid her hairdo to tumble down.

He invites her to join him
in celebrating the late moon, bathing
the world with its magic lantern, the lawn's
wetness and marigolds exuding sweetness.

**Alta – A blushing pink smear for the toes and sides of the soles of the feet that the traditional women of Odisha use to give their feet a tender and nubile look.
*Second sin - an irony the poet uses juxtaposing the first sin, the 'coitus', as believed by the conservative Catholics.

(Part-II)

Fragrant sandal wood haunts the air
these days, you come awash with that scent,
or the perfume of my mad love for you.

My excited words may confuse you
as the glib talk of an obsessive flirt
enamoured by you like a rogue bull.

Don't mind if I refer to the brother's wife,
it's a fig-leaf to camouflage my amour.
Honey, the first rain fills you with its petrichor?

Your doe eyes bring me the repose,
a calmness that would suffuse me in childhood
when my mother used to draw her Rangoli.

Even the grass blades go lush
when you take a walk on them,
as if - you bring them the cool rain,

night dew. They wait for your footfall
with the eagerness of a calf for its mother
like my fancy for meeting the Maker,

who, I recall, has designed the dark clouds,
stealing the kohl from your eyes;

has laced the mornings with the thrills
of the sylvan lush looks,
made the green acres, orchards,

and the tranquil of dusty village lanes
in the template of your coy smiles.
I, a nitwit, bow to you with worshipful love.

(Part-III)

The dirty dishes clamour for attention,
they slip from your unmindful grip.

Morsels of food lose their way
in my abstracted gullet.

A crow caws in raw urgency on the roof top.
Look - the afternoon looms languid.

Do you, honey, feel your blood churn
to a vortex? Does its heat torment the flesh?

As does mine, smarting with an unknown ache?
Or is it all a fancy of my besotted soul?

We try our best to extract
our pound of joy,

the old rusted sky
looming over the muddy earth beneath,

your eyes half shut and half ajar,
confuse me if the pangs of love

dripping down, how far can you walk
with your painful sores.

Would you honey, forgive the last night's dew
that washed clean the *Alta*-blush of your feet?

Wear it again for the sake of my fancy?
Would you dear, re-do your exquisite hair

collecting the tumbled down asps and forgiving
my fickle fingers, and accepting my marigold?

The Goat-Herd Girl
(*Chhelijagali Jhia*)

Don't stamp your feet,
throw tantrums,
no one will paint your feet
with the pink-blush of *Alata*.
Don't drown yourself in tears, poor dearie,
no one will buy you kohl for your eyes.

The half-light of the dawn
is ushering in a daybreak.
Mops have gone busy on floors
to clean-swab the indoors,
brooms have joined them in tandem
to sweep-clean outdoors.
The birds are getting ready
to announce the new day.

They urge you to leave bed, not to
lie lazy in its soft lap, poor dearie.
They poke you to take out
your goats for grazing.
When the goats get grazing, you are
not to lie back and daydream:

your dollhouse days,
that have passed years ago.
Rather live in the present,
the glaring reality, poor dearie.

Rather, let your young eyes mesmerize
the dry twigs to blossom;
the soft touch of your bare feet
turn the barren earth go fertile.
Day dreaming is nor your forte,
poor dear, neither brooding in solitude.

Hitching the sari up,
swinging a free hand,
an unmindful twig
clutched in the other,

you walk with a swagger by the canal.
Is this confidence
you have borrowed from the moon?
Do the green fields smear
their half-smile
on your cupid lips?
Do you steal your sulk
from the frowning black cloud?

While herding goats,
why your mind strays
to the vistas of pipedreams?
Such luxury is a no-no for you.

If the rice-plate,
served to you
by your brother's wife
who tom-toms
of her love for you,
contains rat-shit pellets;
don't grumble, rather be warned.

It still fills your belly,
let you survive,
better than no clean rice-plate.

If your eyes go moist
over the rat-shit in your rice meal,
recall your late loving mother,
recall her own rat-shit life.

Evenings make you forlorn;
you feel sad and bitter.
My counsel, don't reject
the rice-plate containing rat-shit;
it's your legacy, legacy of the poor,
can't be wished away.

You walk back home
by the canal, its water mirroring
the multihued evening;
but the shrubberies
by the sidewalk seem to hide
an insidious dark
in big chunks.

Why does your confidence
sag like a child's,
who is lost in a fair;
why does your face wither?
Is it like the hesitant moon
that broods before setting?
Are you being carried away
by your childhood memories again?

You look for that moon
the adults promised to give you
when you were a kid?
Alas, the promises
are lost and as well
those jovial adults.

Throwing pebbles
into the pond,
with an absent mind;
your brooding visage,
my poor dearie,
give your inner stirrings away;
why to count chickens
before they hatch?

Don't be careless, and
let your goats stray,
don't remain oblivious
to threatening squalls in the sky.

Rather wait for your fortunes
to smile back
when your brother returns
from his long business trip.

Leave bed,
though the sun is not yet up,
though your eyes still feel bleary
with sleep;

rush to the grazing ground
with your herd of goats,

keep humouring
your brother's wily wife;

follow her bidding; poor dear,
she is the bird in hand,
better than many
in the bush.

Wishes are no horses,
no use harnessing them
for your rides,
you are no better than a beggar girl.

Don't throw tantrums,
poor dearie,
don't stamp feet,
don't throw tantrums,

no one gives a damn;
no pedicure or kohl for you
that you can't afford,
take what comes, may it be rat-shit.

Dak Bungalow (*Daakbanglaa*)

Chicken feathers and eggshells
thrown from the kitchen window,
dead flowers from vases,
a soiled bra and panties
of abused nights congest and block

a seedling's green-shoot
from craning out its neck
to take a look
at the free world.

The broken shards
of liquor bottles
shine in the sun, like an irony.
The big room behind hides
skeletons in cupboards.

The old gardener
passes away,
a new incumbent
in his shoes, except that
nothing changes.

The time
does not tick here
unless seasons break the monotony:
the blooms, blossoms and flowers –
Jasmines in winter
Gulmohar in summer.

The power that be
washes hands
of the smell of blood,
muffle ears against shrieks of pain.

As a *Tagara* tree
explodes with white brilliance,
so does a girl
arrives in the big room:

changing into a new sari
discarding her old worn frock.

By the daybreak
the lantern's flame sputters,
tired of the nightlong
deflowering orgy.

Woodworms go rampant
even in daylight,
devouring bamboo rafters,
the façade of protection;
the lukewarm promises
are not worth a fig leaf.

As always,
the timid-most deer
falls prey to the predator,
the big room, a jungle.

A sahib preens
before the mirror
with dentures and
a wig to hoodwink
the poor young girl, and
pamper his own shrunken manhood.

But no one dares
to call off his bluff:
caricaturing youth!
The guard would turn
in pretended sleep, face
the other side and snore.

Ascetics and beggars alike
return empty handed
from this *Daakbanglaa* gate.
Who except the walls of the big room
in this sin-house would
respond to these alms-seekers,
by crumbling from guilt.

The little girl's dreams
of a delightful Diwali
disappear as do
the sloganeering after the election.
The little angel would return home,
if at all, her innocence killed.

Her blood-soaked petticoat
would be howling in pain
thrown into a muck-heap
behind the bungalow.
Mute witnesses –
a Dhatura bush, a gutter.

But the *daakbanglaa* counts the sins,
the time's ultimate reckoner.

How Could The Sea Breach The Trust? (*Samudraku Bishwaasa Naahin*)

A shibboleth: the sea never breaches
its shore, never takes away a thing.
It returns every bit with the ebb
of what's washed away
by its tidal waves.

Isn't that a debunked myth?
As good as an old wives' tale?
Would it give me back
my son
it washed away?

And the cow
that gave us milk?
Prone to her hunger,
she went out grazing.
What of her trust that the sea
would never cross its shore?

Like a thief
it stole away the rice
from inside the paddy pods
of the standing crop,
leaving empty husk
for harvesting.

Its cyclone tonsured
the trees bald, denuded of leaves
but the green foliage
are returning,
also, the birds and bees
that had left.

But the sea is not to be trusted
more than the permanence
of a drop of dew
basking in the morning sun.

A trust breached, a wheel's hub
going askew on its axis,
like a piece of human pinna
in the fish stomach killing the appetite.

The fisher folks these days
fear the sea, it's no more their friend.
It may stealthily rush into
their hutments, forgetting the kinship.

Can it be trusted anymore?
Look at its deadpan visage,
it doesn't bat an eye or burp
even after swallowing all.

A burpless hunger swallowing
men, women and children,
the livestock, food grains
standing crops and
their wherewithal like an
one-way blackhole.

There cries a little kid,
left abandoned and
orphaned by the sea
Would the waves
adopt it?

Would they send
the unfortunate child,
to a school, buy it a pair of
new uniform, and shoes?

(The poem is a reflection in the aftermath of Odisha's Super Cyclone, 1999, devastating the state's East-coast. The sea rose and rushed 35 kilo meters inland, wiping out thousands of villages.)

Home, Sweet Home (*Ghara*)

The sweltering noon at home
brings a sweeping squall,
shaking mango trees
bringing down mango fruitlets
the rising little green nipples
wafting heady-tangy aroma.

The dust storm brings
rolling clouds, black and pregnant,
on its heels; the rain and wind
play snake and ladder.

In normal days, the talkative milk-maid
walks away from the front door
biting a mock-tongue
in embarrassment,
caught red-handed
with watery milk.

The milk-maid
whispers at a crack
at the back door by afternoon
like an intimate accomplice,
"Are you having your forty winks auntie?"

A beehive hangs behind the house,
bees fill it up with honey
from flowers of umpteen flavours
blooming around the village.
The weaver bird stitches a nest
with varieties strands from twigs.

Our boundary fencing
of bamboo rafters
is falling apart,
being old and worn.
Hordes of faceless children arrive
rummaging them for firewood.
They steal away
the sun-dried pieces.

And on a platter, rice-grains
are offered to the birds.
They come crowding,
hundreds of chirping sparrows.

Autumn
(*Sharat Rutu*)

In a white sari, carrying
a basket of white *Tagar**,
autumn arrives in our middle,
startling us. We gasp.
The stings of our sultry sweat
vaporize with its balmy breeze.

Across the clear sky
rainless white puffs float away

the monsoon withdraws,
the pleasant dryness
is unlike a drought doesn't dash hopes,
rather ushers in dreams.

An incrementally growing moon,
from grillwork of cotton clouds,
peeks down with its patchy face.
It looks like smarting in with impatience,
its scabby look, a giveaway of its intent
to put healing balm to the tainted folks.

Her sari like the motley sky and
 the scabbed moon has joyous vibes
with a sad undertone of green-white.
Standing paddy crop ripens
in fields, the farmer planning
for a bountiful harvest.

The rampant weeds, the gift
from a late-departing monsoon,
overpower the farmer's fences merrily,
hedging its strength, mud settles
in rivers, bringing the sparkle back
to their gurgling streams.

For no specific reason,
suddenly the heart feels lonely,
yearning for the beloved,
the cherished closeness
and touch, the pampered hours
in her company and sweet nothings.

Long white-stalked and feathery
*Kasatandi**, blooming like
shy brides of Autumn, 'poesy' in person,
anointed by the setting sun a blushing pink.
How innocuously the white plumes bask red,
negating blood-soaked assassin's hands!

*Gangashiuli**, the night-queen,
celebrates her annual bloom
wafting sweetness around;
palmfuls brought home by my little girl
exude a lingering fragrance
filling us with bonhomie.

The balmy weather
spur the underworld
to unleash their terror.
As well the entertainers -
a circus, its floodlights mixing with
the kitchen smoke, make a halo.

Poor farmers wash-clean
their Sunday best to visit the circus,
may those be vests
out of their boxes, a little
month-eaten, greying, yet,
a proud wear to stand their honesty.

Let the blessed season
gift long life to Mother Teresa,
and Nelson Mandela.
Let their pure souls
get the soothing balm
and the healing touch of Autumn.

I am from 'Mao-Cadre'
(*Mu Mao-Cadre*)

(I)
These hills, jungles,
the nature's bounty
are none of your legacy;
how dare you hand them over
to the scavenging traders,
wheeling dealing in your parlours?

You don't even take
my consent, I,
their real owners.
I therefore turn Naxal, join the Mao-cadre,
take up arms to liberate
my land, restore my rights.

The power and pelf
you enjoy should be mine;
the water in your reservoirs
should irrigate my land,
the jungles you loot
are my inherited property.

Like the Devil
you collect souls
in your creel of lures,
tempting the poor with money;
you moth-hole
our social fabric

like caterpillars
destroying crops.
you eliminate us making us pawns
on your chess board.
I would play with a gambit,
by joining the Mao-cadre;

we would not show you
the real us; hide
behind masks -
we would wash your dishes,
sweep your floors, even our women
may warm your beds;

we send you our sisters,
even play as their pimps,
to sizzle your sexual orgies,
that would be our strategy.
But soon, our masks
would fall off,

startling you
with your pants down;
you would see
the real us –
squat, tough, and tensile
like the desert grass.

We never shed a tear,
our eyes rather smoulder
with the ember of vengeance.
We pack gunpowder

under our skin,
ticking bombs in our ribcages.

We don't accept your rules;
our blood is as corrosive as acid,
would pulp you alive. No jails
on land, in sea, or hills,
high their walls may be,
can confine us.

I, the giant eagle, would crush
the high walls like biscuits
with the flexing of my great wings.
I would be the tinder
for your kegs of powder,
would pulverize you; I am a Naxal.

I would spit in your dinner,
my decapitated head
dripping with blood
would dangle down
the lissom necks of your whores
to drive you cold.

You can't exile me,
I will return, cause
your death knell toll.
I am a seed, ready
to sprout, to sound bugles
for tidings of freedom.

I am from 'Mao-Cadre'
(*Mu Mao-Cadre*)

(II)
Don't blow your fuse if I blow up
a police station, or a railway track;
if my land mines blow up
vehicles carrying your police.

No use banging head
against concrete, or
bleed; see, these
are only mock drills

of a holocaust in the offing
as fearful as *Rudra-Tandav*,
the ultimate destroyer.
I would land on you as one,

with blood-curdling roars,
a bolt from the blue;
would spill your blood
having curdled into reddish water.

Even children and pregnant women
would be sacrificed on the altar
to appease our deity of freedom.
But I would wrap

the naked thighs from
the rape scene with the Tricolour
that might heal the wounds
inflicted by injustice.

I would launch a war
if my people go hungry,
if they don't get a square meal,
or a yard of cloth to protect bare skin.

I would rather die fighting,
my fight would continue
from my deathbed;
your nemesis, your annihilator;

in a war, the ultimate survivor.
From your watch
I would disappear and appear
at my will, I am a Naxal.

Taila's Concept Of His Homeland
(Desha Kahile Jaahaa Bujhe Taila)

Taila helplessly watches – his homeland
passing into the hands of bugbears, ruinous,
of misery and penury. His land's
bloodstains stick to the bogeyman's teeth.
The beast drags his land's rotting carcass
uphill, naming it progress.

Taila, however, would rejoice
a dream-nation of his fancy –
refreshing breath of free air,
a fistful of intimate sky;
a square meal, be it coarse and frugal;
hubbub of loved ones around.

A land, lush and rich with bounties -
herbs, fruits and roots,
abounding with flora and fauna;
mountains, aquamarine and resplendent;
rivers brimming after soothing monsoons;
a sip for one and all for wetting the throat.

In his land, no needy would return
from doorsteps empty-handed,
roads would be safe
for women, and for the meek,
the fickle wind won't even be allowed
to ruffle their poor and scanty wraps.

Taila's patriotic message rings clear –
Love thy neighbour,
never hesitate to lend and borrow
while dealing with borrowing from
or lending to neighbours; or when
sharing your good fortunes with them;

if a pilgrim enroute Amarnath,
or a tourist in an unknown terrain
of Kashmir valley is in distress,
let it be you, an unknown local, who extends
a spontaneous helping hand
like the proverbial good Samaritan;

face your misfortunes bravely
like when pests destroy crops;
compete with others to be
a martyr when the land is in peril,
take the enemy bullet, as if,
those were your beloved's kisses.

An Elegy To My Ruined Crop
(*Oojudaa Khetara Geeta*)

What an ominous night was it!
My lush land turned barren,
neither ravaged by the pariah cattle,
nor trampled by wild elephants.
By morning, it all was gone, the season's
standing crop, the year's breadbasket.

Didn't I invest all in that land,
my flesh and blood included?
Fenced it by the tenacity of my bones
held together with my ligaments,
didn't I toil like an untiring morning-lark,
a song on lips, a shovel in hands.

From my fields, the banana plants
of my kitchen garden
had made a pleasing blur,
a dusty green patch in the ruddy sun
that had tilted down its zenith, my wife's profile
in sari emerging from the village lane.

Then I would see the lunch basket
on her head, heaving my tired body with joy!
Where has all that disappeared: the green potato patches,
dew-drenched bitter gourd creepers, nubile tendrils
of cucumber creepers and the red pumpkins
poking heads up like mice out of their holes?

Neither was there a whirlwind, nor a deluge,
no freakish lightning or fire. Nor a thunder storm,

none knew what ruined my standing crops,
my lush-green lot into a waste-land.
After harvest all my neighboring houses
would resound with the joy, except mine.

My house would resemble a school
during vacation, my harvesting yard
a sulking orphan, jealous of others basking with joy.
The misfortune perching on my roof
like a vulture - a land-tax notice at the door,
the house empty of provisions.

Even my family would not limp through
the lean period, but no brass piece, or gold
to pawn or sell to meet essential expenses.
How did it happen? Neither stray cattle
nor wild elephants, no other disasters,
I stand bereft, poor, ruined, a hapless farmer.

For You, Imraanaa, Only For You
(*Imraanaa, Keval Tumapaain*)

Neither a god, big or small,
nor a prophet, eloquent or silent;
neither a man, nor a woman,
it's me, a humble word-smith.

The moon plays hide-and-seek
among patches of clouds, "Catch me
if you can…", a merry-go-round.
But the game reminds me of a pale hand,

your hand, bloodless and hanging out
of your flower-bedecked coffin.
How does the decoration matter
to your unseeing marble-eyes?

Your subdued *Nikanama* got
drowned by the roar
of a rampant tiger at large,
a two-legged (wo)man-eater.

What time is it, Imraanna?
Night seems unending,
my pretended sleep
is ajar behind closed eyelids.

Lonely nights chase me, urge me
to wake you up from your grave,
take you for a leisurely walk
in silence along the riverbank.

What would we talk about? Almost everything
is a no-no, having lost their relevance.
Don't cry Imraanaa, the tears would
soak your shroud, sobs crush your chest.

Why did you surrender to death
so quietly, Imraanaa, without giving a fight?
Wasn't anyone there by you to help
when the old tiger went berserk

in your bed? Couldn't you find
a shard of broken glass to stab him?

Use your sharp teeth to pull out
his entrails, a woman's ultimate tool?

Might be your husband was looking
for salvation at a country liquor bar,
your *amma*-in-law had gone out
to earn her daily wage, children playing

with marbles out of earshot.
You knew, it would be a waste of time
to ask for help from a hymn-buff Ishwar
or a Namaz-addict Allah, anyway.

Why did these saviors of humanity,
turn a Nelson's eye, when the tiger
ravaged your soft bosoms, muddied
the serene stream between your thighs?

It was like disrobing Panchali
in open *Kuru*-court, like unleashing
a desperado and feeling safe after
putting a few crumbs in his pocket.

The activists shouted slogans,
held candle-marches; the leaders,
visiting to console your family,
slyly groped your minor girls.

Like the weaver bird least bothered
of its nest against the strong wind,
your neighbor Chaitaa, the rickshaw-puller,
visited his routine liquor shop after the day's work.

It is only me, whose head hangs
in shame, as you gave up fight
like the ever-tolerant Sita and sought
your peace in the mother earth's lap.

So, I would invoke you by
the long arm of my pen,
not of law, Imraana, to rise
and fight for your peers in pain.

Neither a god, big or small,
nor a prophet, eloquent or silent;
neither a man, nor a woman,
it's I who invoke, a humble word-smith.

My Big Brother's Wife: Utterly Motherly (*Nuaa'oo*)

(1)
A delicate dewdrop
on a slender paddy leaf,
brings home your memories, *Nuaa'oo**,
soaked in the aroma of sandal paste.

Memories come rushing –
your bangles' muted jangles
filling the dawn as you leave bed,
most of the world still asleep;

except the distant poundings
in the house of *chuda** pounders,

readying the breakfast for the entire village.
You get busy in household chores;

sweeping and swabbing the floors,
washing the dishes, decorating the ground
by drawing the endearing footprints
of the goddess Laxmi to entice her indoors.

It appears the buds on flowering trees,
and marigold plants wait
for opening their eyes until you wake up;
they celebrate exuding their sweetness.

Late night rustles and whispers
from your room softly stir the silent dark;
I wonder what keeps you awake
so late, so cautiously busy.

The mystery thickens by morning
when you blush to my remark,
"You seem to have lost your left anklet.
Where is your right earring and pink hair-clip?"

(*Nuaa'oo** - older brother's wife is addressed by this affectionate salutation. *Chuda** - flattened rice, a staple food item in rural Odia households, taken as snacks.)

(2)
That night she made a paste
of the black gram that her husband
brought from the market, leavened the paste
overnight, and sun-dried them as dumplings.

Our mouths watered for those delicious *vadis**
sauteed in her kitchen, tongues tingled
when aroma wafted around the house
from her chutneys being tempered in pans.

She was ever so worried for the sad fate
of the under-dogs; she worried
for the hungry orphans; her helpless visage
turned sad like the village lanes in afternoons.

We knew her worry would bring milk
to the hungry little mouths, succor
to the poor. It might sound like a joke – but,
she could turn a fallow patch lush garden.

Her care made gnarled trees
blossom, and as if, her wishes made
the bare sky fill with rain clouds.
She could be as generous as the earth.

Her gifts and charity in our lives
are legends, secured and bountiful,
as mother earth's; but if she lost temper,
she could be as angry as the salty tumultuous sea.

(*Vadi** - dumplings from the fermented paste of pulses,
spiced with salt and herbs, and dried for being cooked as
delicacies.)

(3)
Bamboo leaves blowing in the wind
bring you to memory with a broom in hand;
sweeping the backyard by the pond.

We miss you. You come home
with the appetizing aroma
of mango fruitlets, we squeezed
into the delicious *pakhaala**,
made out of softened steamed rice,
lightly seasoned overnight. The riverbank
of Kathjodi is missing your desultory walks;
as does your husband, but differently as a king
would miss his queen on his king-size bed.
He is missing the joy of his life,
your mother-in-law her oil massages
by your hands; and your sister-in-law recalls
how you managed to make her scalp lice-free.

You cared for all, but neglected yourself,
your undone hair blew free with no hairdo,
the wild jasmines in the hedge withered,
waiting for your coif the whole day.

(4)
I go out to sow the field
as pregnant clouds surround the village,
a large cactus flower's whiteness
against the dark sky brings you to mind.

A desolate star feebly twinkles
in my sky after the moon has set.
I go hungry, and feeling like an orphan,
I seek you in that feebleness.

The Struggle
(*Yuddha*)

This is no leavening of dough
for baking bread, your writ won't run,
you are not the ultimate chef
to decide people's choice and taste.

You are no creator, nor curator,
of stars and planets,
no arbiter of their rising
or setting.

Bees hum,
the moon washes the nights
with her milky glow,
blue lilies romance with the sun;

the caressing notes of a flute
fill the evening with ecstasy,
the Mullah's Azan and Pooja bells
and ringing of cymbals affirm, we are alive.

You blast bombs at places of worship,
fill serene evenings with screams of fear;
you wallow in bloodshed with impunity,
aren't you ashamed of your macabre acts?

Simple folks are waiting with bated breath
to watch nymphs, descend into the lake
for frolicking in night's solitude, or gods and
goddesses romance in temple yards,

aglow with little lanterns carried
by fire-flies; but you arrive and blow up
their hopes and dreams,
as if you are the Lord Shiva!

Hadn't it been wise for you
before your irreversible acts of terror
to know that they were ordinary men,
women, and children; no traitors.

Your nightmares make you
insane with rage, hide in bunkers,
ambush and kill them, even Alibaba
and his forty thieves were wiser.

Perhaps, you have a chip on your shoulders
from childhood. Your playmate, a bully,
rode you roughshod; you grew up as a bully
with wounded ego barking up the wrong tree.

God creates the sky for the birds to fly,
spreads meadows before children to
to play and fly kites; but you have usurped
them all, your stentorian preaching

drowns even the sober precepts
of the churches, mosques, and temples.
The air chokes with your loud decibels,
in the shape of hymns and Azans.

You wish the world to bow before you,
cringe at your beck and call;
but soon you would be a sepia page
in history books. Sons of the soil would rule.

How Did You Celebrate Your New Year Day?
(*Kemiti Katilaa Nuaa Varsha*)

(1)
Hey, how did it pass
your New Year Day?
Any New Year's Eve Party?
What of the pre-planned picnic?

It was so sad to hear
about your uncle's death who met
the fatal accident on his way home
from his migrant job site.

No happy tidings this end, friend,
this New Year, wife's rheumatism
getting worse, and son fracturing
a leg in a scooter accident.

(2)
Did you notice a small news report?
It was hiding in an inner page (out of shame?)
of our news daily. It's about the gangrape
and killing of a nine-year-old girl!

Sangita was from our neighbourhood,
studying in third standard. You may recall -
giving her an ice cream candy
during the Vedavyasa Fair, do you?

How helpless she might be
in those cruel hands, choking

her sobs, smothering cries of agony
and shouts for help.

How would anyone hear
her cries, when loud and lewd
movie songs, deafening religious discourses
smother all ears all the time?

(3)

When we visited her,
she lay motionless, blood pouring
out of her cracked head, nose, ears,
and torn and wounded private parts;

her inner garments in shreds,
the design of bees, printed on her frock
no more than cracking coagulated blood
and smears of mud and grime;

the fresh flowers she wore that morning
in her hair looked more crushed than her.
She lay lifeless and stone-deaf,
no response to any solicitations.

(4)

Life this end has gone listless
with Sangita's sordid end,
I have lost appetite. Oh, poetry?
I have put aside that fond hobby.

I seriously ponder over giving up
poetry. My two decades-long efforts
to reform society with my pen
has come around a full circle;

it has failed to save little Sangita
from getting gang-raped and killed
in a crowded locality. We lost her,
my impotent rage is angrier.

Karna

The regular fish vendor
roams our village lanes,
a married woman, wearing a spot
of Kumkum on forehead, bangles on wrists.

She is nameless to villagers,
except her identity as Kata-ma'
(the mother of Kata), an inviolable tie
binding her motherhood to the fore.

Kata-ma's cry, "Would you like
a piece of delicious Hilsa?"
slices the silence like an assurance
to our village, to its stolid serenity.

Another vendor, Anadi, follows suit,
not as frequent, selling assortment
of goods - peacock feathers, Kumkum
and other tidbits; a reassurance for our quiet life.

The childhood is cherished, celebrated
in the village's warm motherly lap;
grows losing the count of time, birds
nest in trees, monsoons visit routinely.

I recall bothering my mother for this and that.
One restful afternoon; she, was cross

with me; pushed me out of her lap,
"Don't harass me, you lucky son of a bitch."

If she said it tongue-in-cheek,
it escaped my kiddish notice. Continued,
"Not my son, you little lucky brute,
I found you lying by the river bank

where your bitch of a mother
had dumped you." My heart broke
to bits to see my village aunts
join her with tch…tch…shaking heads;

I looked out for sympathizers to dispel
my doubt, but our little calf jumped
and ran around with joy to join
the crow, "Yes, son of a bitch, right."

Gecko on the wall also agreed, "Tick tick.
That's right, that's right, you, lucky son of…"
My own Barbie Doll turned her face from me,
even a cicada scurried away into the cesspit.

The words surrounded me, its curse
laying a siege to my loveless air,
like a motherless kid in an alien village
marooned by non-stop rain;

worse than a wood-worm-eaten
discarded bullock-cart
left to rot in a dump
among unwanted odds and ends.

(Mythical Prince Karna, born to unmarried Kunti, abandoned by her, was luckily found and brought up by low-born Radha and Adhiratha, a charioteer. Though restored to power and pelf as a royal born, by Duryodhana as his vasal king of Anga Desha, but always teased by other princes as Sutputra, the son of a charioteer.)

If one Promises the Moon to his Wife... (*Khaali Sinthare Re Janha Padile...*)

If one holds a fistful of sun at Lahore
or Delhi, it looks the same, pale orange.
A splinter of moon nestling
in the parting of the beloved's hair
doesn't look different, may it be
at the shrine of Rahim or Ram.

When a soldier leaves home
for the front, eyes of his loved ones
well up with tears,
wouldn't similar tears be stinging the eyes
across the border? Strange, how
borders fail to sift the grain from chaff!

The soldier gives his word to his wife
and children to return triumphant
with flowers and gifts. He promises
his wife many moons together.
What of his enemy's promise
across the border to his wife?

On the summit of Kargil Hills,
our soldier's bayonet may question him,
"How would you keep your promise
and the honor the words of your enemy?
Isn't he, as worthy a patriot, as you? Doesn't
his wife deserve her moonlit nights with him?"

The moon and your wife
would be waiting your return at Delhi;
and his beside the moon at Lahore.
Both the waiting, balancing the weighing scale,
question the necessity of wars, not simple as killing a bird.
None of you can deny the moon to your wives.

Kamalakanta Panda (Kalpanta)

Kamalakanta Panda (Kalpanta) - A renowned Odia poet lives at and writes from Bhubaneswar, the city of temples, over the last half a century. He is often referred to as Kalpanta (Timelessness) in Odia literary circles. He is a poet of almost legendary repute and if one has not read Kalpanta, then, he hasn't read the quintessence of Odia Poetry. He is famously known for his quirky ideas: not to publish poems as collected works in books, not to subscribe to any social media including WhatsApp, reviving archaic Odia words from the forgotten pages of ancient usages and other quaint decisions. He can be attributed with another distinction like – after a lifetime service to Odia literature and producing genuine and sublime Odia Poetry of the highest standard, none of the arbiters of various literary awards have considered his name for an award or a citation of laurels. (He can be reached at his resident telephone No.06742360394 and his mobile No. 09437390003)

The Song Of Silence (*Nishabd Swara*)

Muted green
of the banana grove
brings me the quiet beats
of your heart;

like shouting of the boatman
brings a relieved sigh
to the worried traveller
waiting to cross a swollen river.

With braille you etch my skin
writing the alphabet of love,
the caressing raindrops
wet-finger the earth,
perfect metaphors for
our private poetry.

Your entry into my life,
a refreshing breeze;
emboldens me against
my sorrows.
Guilts and remorse
bolt by the backdoor.

My heart feels sheltered
in your cloistered love,
you, and my sacred basil,
enshrined in my house,
my presiding deity,
I love to be your captive devotee.

Wish You Well, Sweetheart (*Kalyaani Ichchhaa*)

My heart goes out galloping
in search of you,
across hills and plains
to the snowbound land, hoping

the snow would thaw
into gurgling streams,
wash away
differences, the icy-crust.

Darkness rules my world:
my room, study, the desk;
it roams outside the windows,
chokes my heart's atrium.

Heartbeats hammer my insides,
the garden dims hazy with rolling fog;
the telephone wire lies idle,
does not connect you to me,

a small consolation, rather
concession, makes my eyes moist,
desolation creates a clutter;
scurrying dry leaves in June wind.

Mind remains ajar, agitated,
refusing to doze off;
the morning's refreshing cool breeze
stands helpless, twiddling thumbs.

Hopes and longing keep me awake,
the telephone may jangle,
bringing good tidings.
I pray for your welfare.

Black smoke rises from wet rooftops
in the neighbourhood
after a small shower; have the look
of a heart, smouldering.

Would you return to fill up
my void, even gardens
and orchards, look bereft
awaiting you to explode into blooms.

The Tree
(*Gachha*)

The monkey is our ancient grandpa,
the trees are cousins,
says Darwin.

In their veins flows our culture,
our values as legacy
of giving and loving all.

'Live and let live', the axiom,
'Tolerance and thankfulness' the watchword,
also 'Respect others' oddities' the rules.

The trees raise hands skyward
searching for sober showers
for cleansing the pollution.

Their greenery deserves
its worth, sustains trees' own
and our clean breath.

In changing time, billing and cooing
under shrubbery's sylvan solitude
have turned in favor of air-conditioned confines.

The nature spreads a feast
of unlimited bounties for us, but
we in an orgy of progress cut jungles.

Would the wheels ever turn a full cycle?
Would there be a change of heart?
The green age return with its lure?

The Distances, No More Distant
(*Dura: Sabubele Nuhai Duranta*)

Neither the river nor the mountain
seem distant anymore. Centuries ago
the mountain might be sitting remote,
the river, a brook, prattling at its foothills.

The brook morphed into a stream,
then into a river, flowing to us,
wetting our land's parched throat,
feeding its hunger with fertile silt.

The river brought happy tidings
from the hills, its water getting enriched
with minerals; our land harvesting gold.
Hills and rivers our sentient sentinels, guardian gods.

The river now flows wide, deep, full of fish,
prawns, crabs, other tongue-ticklers.
High tides push the sea to meet us by river route.
Its downstream brings us the mountain sutra.

The hills, river and the sea make
the vertices of a familiar triangle these days,
we humans enjoy the cornucopia of the fecund delta
the joy of idyllic pastures and peace -

Food basket, bird songs, the humming
cicadas in shrubberies, cool breeze
blowing from the river, and the hills bringing
rains, and presenting a new sun every morning.

The distances have shrunk.
The mountains, river and the sea
seem like in our neighborhood,
our hearts beating in tandem with theirs.

The Rains (*Varsha*)
(For Cathleen)

THE RAINS -1
A playful puppy,
the rain, lunges to the lap
of our lawn.
The shower.

You pour on me
your mood's smoldering coals,
joy, passion,
and loud tantrums.

In our bodies' wild terrain,
minds repose
before the heart gallop footloose, keel over
again, and again. And it rains.

Never say - never ever feel -
the innocuous flirting
may breach limits.
And it would rain slivers of lust.

THE RAINS – 2

A sudden hush in your
multi-presence childish hubbub,
cooking mock food in a mock kitchen,
raising a mock family.

None made it happen,
there was no commitment
to keep, it just happened, an unseasonal
shower; did not poor but cooled the earth.

None had asked
for the half-bloomed kisses,
or the floundering flames, but etched
in memory, those would go with me to pyre.

THE RAINS – 3

She comes from an alien land,
the first rain, bringing an aroma,
the petrichor of raw flesh.
Or was I a musk-deer, it is mine?

She enters my parched land
drenching it with passion;
I, starved of love, enter home
to keep a tryst, together.

Who is she? What's her identity?
Could she be a pubescent cloud?
A much-missed shower
that turns body's glades wet and lush?

Or the sweet cornucopia,
the platter of bounties
to the body's eager humus,
wafting maddening scent of Kadamba?

RAINS – 4

The earth, wet and cool,
dust settled, the rains having
a light mood; it's a joy to listen
to her mild tap-dance on the roof.

She makes a call
at the despondent heart's door,
bringing in wet aroma of earth,
trotting about like a musk deer.

She heals the sunburns,
gives the feel of joy of a cow
spared of the butcher's knife, left
in a wet meadow with new grass.

Lovers long for each other,
hearts miss beats over and over
as the lovers meet, make
the rains momentous, unforgettable.

Jagannatha, The Lord of Puri
(*Jagannatha*)

You are the quintessence
for us, your devotees, my Lord,

the determinant of our qualities,
the determiner of our abilities;

the root of all our feelings,
but moot point – we feel you in our self.

Building great hopes without your blessings,
collapses like castles of sand.

Heart's atrium reverberates with your name,
your tranquil gaze fills me with peace.

More I meditate to feel you, to know you,
more remote and mysterious you grow.

I surrender with earnest acceptance,
unconditionally, unflinching devotion.

How can you, Lord, be so indifferent?
It bothers me as an insoluble riddle.

You dangle a mirage before me
in my deserted life, turning nightmarish.

But before long, my peace is restored,
I awake into a refreshing wakefulness.

I see my Ram and my neighbor's Rahim in you,
you define my Alpha and my Omega.

You lord, my faith, my joy, my pain,
the pleasure of living, the bliss of Nirvana.

We thankfully adore you, O' lord,
bask in your compassion, your glory.

Monsoon
(*Varsha*)

Clouds bend double,
extend tender hands,
caress the earth's parched lips,
bringing her to smile.

Its muted rumbles
take care not to ruffle
the earth's timid aching
for the showers.

The rain drops
tickle the earth's underbelly,
barren from the drought,
coaxing her to conceive.

The listless river gets restless,
the sluggish fish hastens to find its mate.
The urge for perpetuating its race
fills it with joy of approaching motherhood.

Green shoots emerge
from the wet earth's womb
after the aridness of summer,
a past to forget after paying its toll.

Love takes off its leash.
The desire grows tumescent.
Body's fever is unleashed,
tiptoes into privacy like a whisper.

Solitude
(*Nirolaa*)

Come on, my friend,
come out of the crowd
of despondent shadows;
articulate the word 'hope'
and sing a line to a future,
loaded with bounties.

May your quest be timid,
may your nights remain grounded
with clipped-wing freedom,
but the daybreak would surely
give you back your wings,
bring to you the morning lark.

Out of your crowded retreat
to the quiet lap of solitude,
the cacophony would give way to
the lovely poetry of love and life,
strummed on heart strings.
Your heaven of joy would arrive.

Cyclone And The Timid Village
(*Jhada: Naadaan Gaan*)

An uneasy calm
roams the village; afraid
that the recent unwelcome guest,
the Super Cyclone, makes a revisit.

The love and affection
showered upon the sufferers
by all and sundry, are maintained
like religious relics, carefully in an aumbry.

The same fate has befallen
to the lavish aid from sympathizers,
the gifts cooling their heels
in ware as a hedging for worse times.

After the cyclone's genocide,
the deserted streets look for
known faces, ears remain attentive
to hear familiar voices.

The bereft bathing-*ghat* by the village pond
gape unfocused at distant narrow paths
taken by women to come for a wash;
the pond is missing their daily dips.

The riverbanks miss the hubbub
of the Kartik Purnima crowd, the little boats
carrying lighted lamps, the ritual at the dawn
reminiscing the Odisha's seafaring trade.

The green pastures miss
the grazing cattle, their trampling hooves,
the frolicking calves at mothers' tits.
So do the empty cowsheds.

The school bell awaits, a deathly silence,
await the hands that rang it,
so does the clean blackboard
for the hands with chalks.

The essential commodities
rain from the sky, dollops of compassion,
clever scavengers loot them
before they reach the needy.

The villagers miss their fish curry
with steamed rice, the betrothed brides
blame the cyclone for delaying nuptials,
the widowed women curse it.

People lose faith in gods, the priests
vie with each other for attention.
Devotees and the shorn trees alike,
suffocate with death's stench.

The village can't find itself
on the map. Did it really exist?
Has it retained its identity? Is this all
a déjà vu? A void on the land record?

Corona
(*Karona*)

Exiled to a 'siege within'
we crouch at home, our sobs
dare not heave out,
our cries are swallowed back.

The bogeyman in various guises
roams in our empty lane
looking at the shut doors.
He carries a big bag to collect the souls.

Last night, I talked to a friend
in another city over phone,
that surprisingly made me feel free.
He cried, sobbed and laughed freely.

His laughs and tears,
acceptance of the reality,
drove away my desolation,
vicelike grip of the fear.

Across the closed windows
float about memories,
puffs of cotton clouds. Sweet reveries
of pains and happy tears.

Indoors, lurk our cringing fears,
the dark dungeon of our make.
Outdoors, dance bright days,
Carefree freedom or jail, we to choose.

Would we ever forgive
this invisible predator? Accept it
as a guest, arrived unannounced?
Laugh at its deathly costume as fancy?

A Rollcall for Saora
(*Saooraa*! Saooraa!!*)

A fire consumes the garbage dump.
An effigy of Ravana goes up in flames
to mark the conclusion of Dussehra.
Both the fires aim at
the warding off the Devil,
rather than a spring-cleaning.

The autumn has set in,
night has a nip in the air,
some dew, some leaf fall.

Ravana burns and the people watch
their own guilt burning in its recesses.
None feel as confident as his outer mask.
They keep twiddling thumbs
feeling the cleansing heat inside.

Does the ritual fire burn the sins
committed in cold blood?
The sins deliberately committed
all the time?

But a *Saora* is of a different mold,
cast from a rust-free alloy,

with confident and fair psyche,
of unwavering mettle.
He fought Ravana, the abductor of Sita,
in Ram's Vanar Sena*.

Amazing is a *Saora*'s mind!
Blessed is his soul!
His courage legendary,
archery infallible!
An epitome of the 'virtue',
his lexicon has no room for a 'Lie'.

Alas! Had a *Saora* been around
to fend the little angel
when demoniac lechery
was spilling her blood at Rourkela;

to save the sisters at Baliapal
getting torn asunder
by savages in the garb of reformer;

to stop the looting
of their flesh, blood and honor.

A *Saora*'s absence
was conspicuous
at the desolate Chandaka*,
on January 9th, 1999.
The jungle wept,
the trees and creepers drooped,
hung head in shame.

A *Saora* would have faced the molesters,
challenged the leering bystanders,
guiltier than the guilty.
A *Saora* would have awakened
their comatose conscience.

A Saora would have taught a thing or two
to Guru Drona of unparalleled-archery-fame,
the mute witness to Draupadi's disrobing.

Some spine to the spineless Guru,
some pride to his shameless disciples.

He would have questioned,
"Can you ever repair
a torn honor,
stop the welling up tears?

"Why don't you disarm the Devils?
Can you bring the divine twins,
the medicine men of the gods,
the Ashwini Kumaras,
to heal the wounded earth?

"Isn't Ganga too unequal to wash
the stains of shame, red as blood?"

Not the monsoon rain,
nor the winter's chill
may cool the smoldering soul
of the righteous Saora-anger.

The Ravana is growing, a luxuriant plant
in the sordid mud of human mind.
A Saora of courage and intent is the need
of the hour to annihilate
the Ravana from the roots.

It is time, every man and woman
turn Saora, turn a leaf in Saora lore,
be a brave heart, truthful as a child,
a zealot, a fighter against the oppressors,
annihilating the Ravana, inside, outside.

(*SAOORAA** (Saora) tribe is a part of the widespread *Kandha* community of Adivasi origin, settled in southern parts of Odisha and northern parts of the adjacent Andhra Pradesh. The people of this community are natural archers, famously reputed for their honesty, bravery, justice, and altruistic nature. Chandaka* is a forest that spans between the cities of Cuttack and Bhubaneswar.)

You
(*Tume*)

My restless inner being is missing you.
The air pauses with impatience.
Branches and the twigs
awash with your fragrant memory.

Conspicuous by your absence,
the void murmurs, as well
the distant sea, its vastness, sing
our intimate hours, as unfathomable.

A longing suffuses the soul.
Yearnings dig an empty pit in heart.
The dark interior,
the thin sunbeam on a blackboard,
its soft chalk scribbling
sweet nothings.

Our tender love,
your smiling lips
parted in a pout
in wait, in tremulous desire.

A pervading wish of ours
to plant a *Kalpataru*,
the divine sapling of blessing,
in your garden for the fulfillment
of our wishes, brings me
your engaging smile.

The Cyclone, Mango Tree, And Poet Jayanta Mahapatra
(*Jhada, Aambagachha, Ebang Kavi Jayanta Mahapatra*)

All the curses
would be absolved
by the grand old tree, its branches,
arms raised in benediction.

The stifling suffocation
inside the house

would seek relief from cool breeze
under its refreshing spread.

The old mango-tree
stood with arms raised
posturing as a father offering a hug,
for relief from the bothersome tickling.

Family squabbles would vanish
to see its blossoms. Bruises and scars
would heal watching the hurrying ants
nesting in the folds of its green foliage.

It murmured poetry
amid its tremulous leaves.
Melody seemed to host
all who came beneath its lush invite.

That night of all evil nights,
an unforeseen cyclone shook awoke
its nesting crows, scurrying ants,
filling the dark with violent fury.

The scary bird cry,
the darkness looking for shelter,
the wind, a rampant, rogue tusker;
the tree fought, struggled, but finally fell.

With it fell memories,
visions, poetry, and pain,
sweet hopes of reunions
after partings and hope of creation.

But how carefully it fell,
a mother saving her children,
it crashed and fell so delicately,
keeping the poet's old house

out of its way. Jayanta looks
unfocused at the vacant sky
where stood the old patriarch
holding the family umbrella in all weathers.

He looks ahead to the elegiac lines
that would perhaps pour down his fingers
onto a page for the family-senior,
that so lovingly spared his dwelling

(The Super Cyclone of 1999, that devastated India's east coast, took the toll of the old and big mango tree in the front yard of the poet Jayanta Mahapatra. The tree was dear to many of the master's poet friends.)
***.

Prabhanjan K. Mishra

Prabhanjan K. Mishra, the former president of Poetry Circle of Mumbai, former editor of this poet association's literary journal 'Poiesis', an award-winning poet, writes in a supple style both in Odia and English, using metaphors, symbols, motifs, mainly of Indian association. His poems are replete with mild satire and irony. He generally writes on interpersonal relationship, landscapes, and social dichotomy. His literary politics leans towards the dregs of the society, the dispossessed mass. He is a poet, translator, short story writer, critic, essayist and editor. Poetry is his first creative love. He has three books of poems to his credit and his poems and translations have been included in more than twenty anthologies.

Father: Nostalgia (*Atita*)

Mother sits on her haunches dozing
in sweltering heat on our back verandah,
overlooking our river Sapua,
waiting for father to come to lunch;
her own midday meal would follow his,
a habit of forty years.

In our village cremation ground,
the patch of father's last journey
bears no sign of a month-old pyre
except looking a bit ashy grey

among the weeds, mottled grass;
his pyre has rather shifted to mother's eyes.

Mother looks at the river bank
craning her scrawny neck -
Has he finished his three habitual dips?
She allows only him to judge
her cooking excellence, so, the meowing
hungry cat gets her wagging tongue.

Father had gone on our shoulders,
returned as a bit of ash in an urn;
for mother, an urnful of empty sky,
listless coconut fronds, afternoon's
held breath. The tick tock clock
has died on the wall, and her time frozen.

A toy horse father had brought home
stopped swinging, froze in mid-trot.
Mother found a compatriot
in its stillness. None of them ever came alive;
she joining the toy by a hyphen.
Both seem aspiring for a full stop.

Mother was a mirror-addict,
fastidious about what
the reflections said about her.
Today, she flings grey curses at the mirror.
Grumbles before his photograph about
her mouth tasting like dust-ridden cobweb.

At the sunset, she mumbles, "He would
finish his work, return home early.

I hear him clearing his throat
by the river bank. Would be home
any minute. Let me rush, cook rice,
give dal a ginger-*tadka**; mash a potato..."

"Listen." she insists,
"He is taking a wash
by our backyard well,
singing hymns. No, it's not his brother
whose voice is thinner... No, I don't
believe in ghosts or spirits."

(Ginger-*tadka**: a cooked lentil dal is given a ginger tempering.)

Heart: A Window (*Jharakaa*)

With tousled hair
like wild weeds
across the window, you perch
on window's ledge,
wearing a frosted look in eyes.

You lift a bare arm,
the air goes berserk
beneath your underarm.
Goose-bumps tickle
my wild desire, choking.

The primal hunger
spreads wings, a slow fire
in the underbelly. Hot breath

rises from my teacup,
gasps escape from my lips.

In idle winter
nestles the late afternoon,
a nip in the air;
the plants in pots doze
under the stooping sunrays.

The evening is arriving
bringing the message of jasmines,
my fingers itch for a poem,
the words rise in murmuration,
starlings in our vitreous sky.

Little birds of desire,
swarming our cloistered loneliness,
spread wings between you and me.
A disturbing stillness,
an evening with a difference.

Along river Kua-khai's languid stream
you seem adrift, a rudderless boat
without oarsman, perhaps, looking for
a mooring point. An oxymoron
like our separated togetherness!

Now, I may get up, bring you
some crumbs of words,
in an alphabet soup for your
fastidious taste. My word-crumbs may
meander like tourists in an alien town.

Wish, under the white sheets
our lazy evenings
join palms, bring home
interwoven fingers, our past,
melt our heart-lines and fuse.

Snapshots from Dawn (*Godhuliru*)

In bed, he would put into his little mouth
a shrunken fig from grandma's chest,
her undone grey strands
playing like a lullaby over his visage.

In a terrace corner, he would join
his friend Gunjan, play family,
imitating adults. She, his wife,
pretending to go to bed with him,

delivering children, her dolls.
He ploughing and irrigating the fields,
sowing seeds and waiting patiently
for flowering, fruition and harvest.

Contented, tired, he would go back
to the cool sanctum of grandma's bosom.
At times, parents' bed
would be his endearing retreat.

He felt secure to hear
his mother whispering into dark,
"O dear, it feels heavenly."
That would lull him to sleep.

But some nights, visited by
nightmares, he would feel
guilty of playing 'family'
with his female friend, Gunjan;

feel guilty of eavesdropping
on his parents in bed;
but would dream and urinate happily
into grandma's lap, his ultimate cesspit.

Purposeless
(*Niraadhaara*)

This lovemaking seems cursed,
its commitment a betrayal.
Rapid gallop of our hearts
gives away the guised lust,
as do the tadpoles down the drain.

The Ursa Major questions
our snow-white stance;
it doesn't measure
to Devi Saraswati's purity
or her marble-white swan.

Rather, naked Swati, psychic,
balancing even during twirls
like that in *Kathak* every night,
ignoring the Ursa Major's
raised highbrows, snubbing snorts.

Perhaps, our intent is clear,
our hearts swell up
with ballooning hopes,
but its helium won't
sustain zeppelin hopes.

What of flying the future
like a kite at the end of a rope?
There is no magic carpet in it
for our kids, a miserable lot driving
looking in the rearview mirror!

The gods in heaven are not
celebrating our union as sacred
with drumbeats or
showering heavenly *Parijata* petals
on our bed, no different than a brothel.

This evening is not leading us
to a night of repose and peace,
but to a darkness that would stalk
us to our bed soliciting passions
giving birth at its gross thighs

unplanned children
ending up in quarries,
flesh market, selling for
a few quids, growing old
before living as children.

U-Turn
(*Leutaani*)

The night snores peacefully
on the wake of happy hours,
breathing the sweetness
of contented lassitude,

dreaming in the balmy autumn,
the murmuring leaf-fall,
the rustling wind, languor filling
the bones with lethargy.

Night jasmines waft
their heady fragrance,
the smiling moon hangs like
a nude painting over the hedge.

A dream dances on night's eyelashes;
its feather-touch footwork tickles flesh.
Sweat in your undone hair, the sky
is eagerly getting down on the earth.

The dream's dance is raw and slow,
intoxicated by *Kadamba* smell,
Yamuna's reminiscent spates,
unseasonal rains, joyous showers.

The earth yearns to suck in
her night-love, the downpour,
yearns to get soaking-wet.
The embryos astir in seeds.

Time takes U-turns, repeats,
looks behind, can't keep still,
the passion raises its hood, bites, subsides
into genuflection, again and again.

The past rises resplendent
from its ruins, the shadows
emerge as wild desires
resurrected from the dead.

This nameless night-stand,
the wide-awake somnolence,
its barren past hidden away
behind a fertile monsoon in the past.

The moon unfurls rainbow colors,
stands witness to the fertility dream;
even the conscience, tempered
with discipline, the night behaves smitten.

Pushing a Hurtling Cart, The Time (*Ghaagadaa Samaya Theli*)

No river is too vast to be sucked in
by the sea. Even the proud sea
was gulped down by the frail Rishi Agastya.

Why should the life
feel scared of flowing, afraid
of an unknown new day?

Why should one look for
God's dwelling in temple premises, or
look for Him in Aum's resonance?

No salvation is really traded
in streets of Rome, Mecca or Banaras,
not peddled on the banks of Ganga.

Isn't death the last truth?
The dignified end? Why do we try
to skirt around this inevitability?

Pyramids and the Nile stand witness
to pharaohs' immortality dreams decaying.
Phoenix rises from ashes in metaphors only.

The wounded Konark's wheels
would not defy the time's rust,
would never rush to Jagannath Puri.

The great Vindhya divides
our peninsula into a cultural binary;
let's accept its irretrievable beauty.

Corpses of glorious Kalinga War
would never rise from their pyre,
if Swargadwara cries tons of tears….

May a proud river boast
of its own vast sweetness but the sea
swallows it into its burpless salinity.

The time is not wounded, only tired,
holds its patience, puts perseverance,
a slow-moving hour-hand ticks ahead.

Night Vigil
(*Raati Khoje*)

The night passes open-eyed,
keeping the doors ajar,
digging nails into skin
of the idle bed, looking for

the night-flowers from your hair
rioting with the sweat of your
underbelly, coils of dark frailty;
my eyes go wet with a loss.

Armfuls of your memory
loaded with our soulful past
open-up. Knotted passions
blooming as unseasonal flowers.

But nothing works, I resign;
a defeated king abdicating,
like a tuft of grass, that loses color, dies
lying long beneath a stone's underbelly.

Late nights return with bloodless pallor,
recalling our love, you laying down arms
before the final bell, I running away
from the ring, both ruing our own pride.

Back in memories' lane, your sari
fluttering against the blue sky,
your ankle-bells singing to birds,
nose-diamond winking at stars.

I recall the last drizzle with you,
the deodars by our house,
wet as your curls in raw sweat,
breath as moist as the billowing mist.

Commitment (*Pratishruti*)

In my thought you lie down
languorously in
a contented afternoon,
my bovine hunger chewing cud,
after sumptuous grazing.

Life seems committed never to end
a prisoner's promise to wife
to return soon, as unreal as
the time's assurance
to wait for me and you.

Ours was a nomadic tent
pitched temporarily as shifting
desert dunes, we looking for an oasis,
palm fronds, a cool articulate brook
our best of karma could not commit.

My days behave fickle
like a well-endowed fair woman;

none can unequivocally
claim her affection beyond the whiffs
of her scented scarves.

Nights are not less treacherous,
they keep measuring their mischief
against the days' innocent sins,
they bring back the lost fear,
the forgotten apprehensions.

When a day is in a live-in relationship
with the night, called 'dawn' or 'dusk',
I look for you, the assurance
in your eyes. In those deciding hours,
I love to be committed.

Grey Sorrow: Salty Tears
(Maatiaa Dukha, Luniaa Luha)

Ganpati, sitting at our gate,
trouble-shoots for family,
Jesus, the host of our house,
welcomes all with open arms.

Lakshmi and Sarasvati
balance the indoors and inmates,
weighing learning and lucre
in a crosshair tight rope-walk.

I count Krishna's holy name
on a string of basil bids, carry Quran
in my sling bag, spin yarns
on Bapu's charkha, my peace-accessories.

But a spark spurs my blood
to its flash point,
I defile and break shrines
suiting the occasion, spill blood.

My blind lava flows amok.
I lynch, loot, spread arson;
the predator in me
out of its suave cage.
.
Is my humility,
a façade to look human?
Why do I go berserk
over Ram as well as Rahim?

My people endlessly wait
for the fights to end.
Parents wait for us, the children,
to return home, learn to earn.

Our wives wait to cuddle
their tiny tots yet unborn.
Their breasts droop
waiting for our return.

Aging Monalisa
(Monalisa)

The smiles in your fifties shoot
more lethal arrows than yours in twenties;
your bosoms, powerhouses,
the tips, brandishing daggers.
A Ganga's dichotomy, holy and turbid.

Your intent from its patient lair
for reaping the best of harvests
from sowing till raising a crop,
mesmerizes me as does the opium
of your words to all.

I labor hard, a *Parth* of the *Kali Yug*
pulling the spineless bow to avenge
his *Panchali's un*-coiffed hair,
the flag atop my chariot doesn't flutter,
battle ground, bereft of warriors and bugles.

An aging *Parth*, goes spiritual,
goes fatalist, accepting the wilted garland
of victory from your hands, my wife.
All pretences may die pathetic deaths,
planets may constellate as excuses.

Digging the enigma of your smiles
to find the cipher to my fate,
I find an infertile seed at its
fathomless core, after dives
into your body's humus all my life.

The Skin-Deep Fame
(*Gourabara Patala Chamatale*)

Tired of clearing cobwebs -
Lies and falsehood rule the roost.
Sleight of hand hoodwinks fair deals
with counterfeit compassion.

The rich and poor,
from men of power to those
humbled by fate and birth,
dance for immortality, vainglory.

Force and humility in a mix,
sin with the tempering
of impunity and charity
score the highest number of goals.

Two hoots to monstrous blunders
or irreparable loss to others!
Ingratiating submission of the exploited,
conceals the agenda behind blessings

Most of our portals lie half-built,
the holy sites strewn with rubbles,
the edifices of glory cracking at hips,
reality makes room for fairy tales.

Showcasing hollow promises,
ruining the Holy Ganga
with cleaning budget, sweeping
into it the pyres, gutters and drains.

The waist-belts support our weak spines.
Headgears conceal baldness.
Dentures dazzle over the teeth-loss.
God! When would these vanity fairs stop?

Runu Mohanty

Runu Mohanty interweaves bhakti with sensuality. She does the trick with ease like many Bhakti Era Poets, such as the twelfth century poet Jayadev of Gita Govinda fame and the Tamil poetess Andal of eighth century, elevated to the level of a goddess by her charmed readers. One finds tresses of Rabindranath Tagore in her work. Quite a few are conceived in a style of confessional poetry, and taking parallels from the recent past, the iconic poet Kamala Das. Like Kamala Das, her poems often rub viscerally with sensual expressions. Her dominant themes are 'love', 'surrender' 'devotion' and 'feminine dignity'. She writes with a passion, unique to her, signified with an indelible personal signature.

The Painting Studio (*Chitrashaalaa*)

Not easy for me
to color the reflections,
put pigments
on a bird in flight.

Not easy to paint the flight
of a caged bird to freedom,
equally difficult to paint
a garden bursting into bloom.

As difficult as bringing
paradise to earth, twirling feelings
around a finger; as hard
as making a home.

Drumming under the water,
Ivory palaces,
castles in the air
are fanciful fairytales!

When the soil is fertile, wet,
ready for seeding, why should I
worry over reaping
a green harvest?

I would join my Lord,
may it be his humble hovel
or a grand mansion, if he
indulges my supplications.

My needs are frugal,
though I love luxuriating in plenty.
I manage with a single fruit, though
would love to have in abundance.

I need only a few
of those fulfillments
in my humble sari-corner.
But for my other needs

I cling to my God
like a creeper
clutching him
in utter surrender.

The Whore
(*Ganika*)

She has no name, just an existence,
the flower may bloom
in hutments, or upmarket settlements
with equal abandon.

She is a temptress with frills
and thrills: bewitching kohl
in eyes, pink-dyed palms and soles,
smelling of spring blossoms.

A river with strong undercurrents,
tributaries pouring in,
charming assets, silt of wealth,
un-sedimented promises.

Her heart never in a bind,
a desire: unadulterated, ascetic;
rippling surface, calm depths; a goddess
of fire that enchants and burnishes.

Her words tangle with one's senses
like a gossamer net around a fish
pulling it into her sinuous stream
rippling beneath her slippery silks.

An enchanting *Kadamba* blooms
in her yard, all seasons. All her evenings
wear a magical moon in the sky.
A sizzling silver lining leavening dark-clouds.

She wishes that her company might augur well
for her companions, never ill,
she adorns the bereft thrones in their hearts,
hardly giving away herself, too fastidious a chooser.

Rueful smiles respond to
the blame games: 'a honeytrap',
leaving the choice to her lovers
to drink the honey or the poison.

A wild bloom to her honey bees.
A spot-on hot iron crucible,
malleable unlike the rigid steel;
she shapes herself to her guests' will.

No miser like a catacomb
that receives dead souls. No Blackhole
that takes in all, gives back nothing.
Rather a generous river with life-giving water.

Free, yet besieged, an enchantress
held as a hostage, a ransom
she pays with entertaining
her guests, admirers. A gem in a vault.

A Sybil of esoteric wisdom:
a haven to sinners,
a pilgrimage to seekers,
a punching bag to critics.

she gets immolated
every night, taming the lech,
but remaining untouched by desires,
theirs or of her own, a Buddha.

The Woman
(*Nari*)

She packs a bundle of riddles,
it is euphemized as difficult to decipher -
a princess, a beggar, Rita, Geeta, Sita!
Holds her cards close to her chest,
she only knows the man who strums
her heart's sitar, makes her sing like a canary.

Needs no bed of roses
for her forty winks,
no palatial abode to luxuriate in,
but a bower of her man's adoration;
it's her reliquary, her arbor of life,
her paradise on earth.

No night-creature
not a bundle of naked desires,
never at the beck and call of flesh,
not an unholy grail offering
poison-wine with deceptive sparkle,
her love not requited on a sleazy bed.

Purity of a woman is a holy smoke -
a much tom-tom-ed myth,
a fake benchmark woven around
the virgin blood, a shroud of lies,
the emperor's magical cloak.
Her committed love, her only hallmark.

A devotee, her lover her lord;
her man, the God of her worldly worship.

She heaps her indulgence on her beloved,
ties herself to him with the holy strings,
she is his priestess, his partner; they
complement and supplement each other.

Ektara

My mentor spreads
his security net over me,
his heart goes berserk
to see me in tears,
I rule his heart; my entreaties
are his commands!

It sounds like twigs
breaking underfoot,
the cacophony of people.
The *Ektara** rises above the hubbub,
comes floating to me
riding the *Marua** fragrance.

Someone is dancing
wearing ankle-bells,
his peacock feathers look radiant
stuck into his headgear,
I live and die in his love.
His looks of deep blue mountains.

I go weak on my knees,
forgetting my womanly pride.
I read a few pages
on grammar of love,

learn new words, finer nuances
from his lexicon of passion.

A bird knows its passage of flight,
a river chooses its course
slitting the earth's thighs at its softest,
my love is not reflected in mirrors
but my face, none except he
can fathom and chart it.

Others, possibly grope blindly
the shape of an elephant in the room.
Let the stars twinkle,
the moon shine resplendent,
the flowers bloom in celebration,
the *Ektara* strum and hum awash with love.

They worship the sensual,
they worship the grandeur of death,
take offerings to an orphaned god
lying abandoned in a nameless ruin,
not knowing the bliss of surrender,
not knowing – love is not easy as fame.

Marua – a variety of sacred Basil plant. *Ektara* – the one-string strumming musical instrument.

The Adoration
(*Vandanaa*)

I adore this night.
It may not be the same tomorrow.

I beg, give me your lips,
let me take an eyeful of you,
feed you my wild berries,
take you into my little cottage
decorated with peacock feathers.

My heart is jubilant like a swan's
swaying in rhythm on ripples,
water mirroring its pristine image
in myriad fragments.

I adore the trees
along with their companions –
their foliage and blooms,
the river that soaks their roots
and the clouds
that wash them green.

The wind by the sea would
be in my adoration, the breakers
they bring ashore; they keep
haunting me, my sweet reveries.
I would surrender myself
to this moment, rejoice its bliss.

Tonight, I would adore
my companion with a garland,

let him lead me to light
from the darkness.

Tonight, I would not adore
the gods, not count beads
in their names. it is our night
of adoration, I and my mate.

The Prayer
(*Prarthana*)

My praying limbs may blister,
making me a handicap
but my soul be burnished
by your cleansing fire.

My dreams may die,
please lord, keep my heart alive,
let it keep beating to your love,
your signature bloom in my garden.

Without a voice,
let our souls unite,
be tied in a knot, as lasting
as the one tied by 'Gordius'.

Life-threatening sorrows
deluge me, lord,
bless our love to be immortal;
let tears dissolve heart's barriers.

I do not believe
in 'wearing one's heart
on one's sleeve' as a show off,
it wounds my soul.

Let our bond under
the relentless social hammer
prove itself tough,
a piece of diamond;

but our souls cherish
love's delicacy
softer than the
softest rose petals.

The flesh may decay,
the spirit should soar high;
in pain and hurt;
let not the path lose its way;

let our love keep
us enchanted in its magic,
let not the moon beams
lose their charm in our life.

Oh lord, if you decide
to leave me to my devices;
pray, let not my beloved
leave my side, my heart lonely.

Manali*

Would Manali be busy
so early in this morning?
Would she be plucking
sweet wild berries
from the jungle?

Sitting by purring brooks
and throwing pebbles
into the ripples, submerged
in reverie of the beloved?
Might be winging on wild creepers.

Could she be taking an early bath
in the river Vyas, perching
languidly on a rock by the water?
Could she be chewing a paan,
sweet and scented, and one for the beloved?

She might be stringing
wild roses for God
in her Goshal village.
Wonder, what could be
occupying her this morning!

The rising sun behind the hills,
the pears ripening in slim arms
of the trees in orchards,
the shadows playing tricks
with the morning light.

The streams' vaporous breaths,
chirruping birds singing on trees;
do they compete with the sun,
hills, wind and clouds
for Manali's attention?

Do even fleeting butterflies,
the furry rabbits, roly-poly puffs
of the cold mist also compete
to find space in the daily rainbow
of Manali's morning schedule?

And lo, an unknown poet
living by the seashore of Puri,
thousands of miles away,
tries to capture Manali
in a humble poem, and her memories!

And the lovely
the ever-young princess Manali
reposes in her languorous hillside,
making her home
a pride of her land.

(Manali* - The hill station.)

The Flight
(*Oodaan*)

Take shelter in a stranger's house
in an unforeseen rain,
shut doors and windows
against squalls and gusty winds,

sweep the sharp splinters off the floor
before they wound your feet,
take care of the situation before
the pressure in mind's cooker bursts.

A bird in a cage is no bird,
a bird without flight is unhappy,
know the art of disrobing,
don't wait until the robe is on fire.

Life is sorrow, hurt and pain
come in wagon-loads,
fill the spaces from birth to death.
Some pain is very personal –

its privacy can't be shared with any,
like coming out of the neck-deep water
without clothes. The shame is chillier,
than the water, with another excuse.

Don't go mad, if you can't
push a hill out of your way,
don't act weird, be a social animal,
reap its benefits. Don't run naked.

Don't beautify the ugly,
it may turn uglier. Worship the body,
its tell-tale details. Get rid of the wetness,
shame, but not by walking in the buff.

God's house is known
by its religious insignia -
a saffron flag, a top-wheel, a cross,
or a star inside a crescent moon.

A woman in love is known
in or out of marriage
from the pure pink roses
blooming on her cheeks.

The Divine Union
(*Mahaa Yoga*)

In matters of love,
rare are the people
born with silver spoons....
the queen bee only privy
to flowers with honey-cores.

From a king to the cowherd
who does not take his partner
to bed? Be it the bed of opulence,
be it the field with standing crop,
be it a roadside inn for travelers!

Love tastes divine either on a houseboat,
or the lush country side arbor, a dreary desert dune;
weaves its nest like the weaver bird,
interlacing every turn and twist of the life's loops,
redolent with the fragrance of union.

Path to the supreme is laid
along the way of a pristine union.
Love rules eternal; is the last residue
after sifting, boiling and filtering;
a glue that joins two souls seamlessly.

Ecstasy in the love's plateau,
bliss in love's peak – they sing hosanna to it
in every land, through civilizations;
none is immune to its magic, its mystique.
It brings kings to their humble knees.

Queens kissing the humble feet
of their slaves; the ultimate equalizer.
All are its slaves - from high
to low, from kings to beggars -
licking the saucer of its joy.

Love is earthy - down to earth,
Steamy, animal, also innocent,
a blessing in our uneven sojourn
through the earth, gifting us -
rock and roll, relish and cherish.

Making love is like worship;
the giggles of joy, howl
of painful pleasure; all leading to
an ultimate silence - a pilgrimage.
An epiphany, a communion with the divine.

Fair-Weather
(*Bhala Paaga*)

A loving companion in a lovely milieu
adds *joie de vivre* to the fair-weather;
you climb the highest of peaks,
hoist your flag on the top of the world.

Start the ritual with adoration
and worship. Learn through experience
the fine art of loving; you need
no baptism, holy dips or doctrines.

Make placid surfaces
dance with ripples under you,
move with strategies, no less intricate
than moving a die in a game of dice.

Pick and choose the signals,
good omens, propitiate moments,
hasten your fingers like on *mridang*s*,
don't you dare losing the rhythms.

Let the fallow land be tilled,
let the fruits be squeezed
until the last drop is spilled. Dear me,
it's not easy to climb to the peak.

You create a history of sorts,
no nocturnal stage performance
that downs its curtains before the dawn.
The curtains once parted, the show must go on.

Like playing a *mridang* continually,
the army's morning regimen of 'left-right',
keep the protagonists battle-fit,
but no tinkering with love's mystique.

Footnote – *Mridang**, is a percussion musical instrument
like *dholak* played with both palms.

A Sufi Song
(Sufi Geeta)

The lamp burns bright, luminous.
The water lies calm, no tide, no ebb.
My sacrifices lie listless.
Has my muse deserted me?

If the green shoot is withering
before raising its head, it's no joke.
I put the right spell to induce its silence
to shine and sing like the goddess Matangi*.

I remain a nonconformist,
refusing to walk the beaten path;
my purity is questioned; am called
a fallen woman wallowing in sin.

I am lost in a jungle,
you may find me, my lord,
as a river in spate
in a moonlit night,

the union should not be orphaned.
 Oh! Give me a break, I will teach you all -

what makes a holy confluence,
what consecrates the desecrated shrine.

The lamp of love dispels
the virulent darkness of lust.
The former enriches in benign radiance,
the latter suffocates, is scorched.

Love is as resilient as the soul,
unlike a mansion that crumbles with age,
unlike an attire that goes
to shreds by overuse.

Eternal as the sea, the wind,
eternal as the Atash Behram* of Udvada.
Its songs are serene
as the melody of purring streams,

the murmur of leaves,
the distant enchanting echo
of a frothing swollen sea,
soothing as the cicada's solo.

My love rejoices in its own halo,
no less holy than the attraction
of the moon for the sea, or
of the aborigine Sabari for Ram.

No less than the pure
sensuality between
the ancient yoginis and yogis
in their quest for Kundalini.

This celebration of love
is worth the prayer in a shrine,
with holy offerings and hymns,
planting the seeds of nirvana.

Footnote – Matangi* is one of the ten Mahavidyas (goddesses) in Tantric tradition; she is equivalent to Sarasvati, the Hindu goddess of music and learning. Atash Behram*, is the eternal sacred fire of Parsees burning at Udvada, Gujarat. The fire was brought by fire-worshipper Parsees when they fled Iran for India during the British era.

The Story Of A Moonlit Night (*Jahna Raati Kathaa*)

Stars, the palm grove, the sea, and the soil
stood witnesses to our union,
joined by the night birds, the moonbeams,
and a lethargic moth suddenly high on wings;
all sang the language of love.

The love was being celebrated
between a flower and a bee; we,
the mere protagonists, only flagged it off.
Even the rising sea didn't
dare to drown our truth.

The scandal and gossip
were our neighbors, spreading
the news of our secret love, as a curse,
an earthquake of sorts, neither partisan
to its victims, or own unleashing.

Love infects all,
even "The holier than thou" ones;
humble sweepers, billionaires,
the Sabari, of the Lord Ram fame.

Who says, "Love's passion
has no virtue" or
"It's not righteous"?
Must be the words of a false messiah.

Even Indra, the King of gods,
chooses Urvashi, the celestial nautch-girl,
over his royal consort *Indrani*
to flirt with, tie a knot of affection.

Love is magical and angelic,
the only charm,
that holds two souls in thrall,
take deeper dips beyond water, mud.

It takes lovers to the buried treasure trove.
Teaches them walk the primitive jungles,
cross treacherous hill passes,
boat across mighty rivers.

They row through Sindhu, Sutlej,
and Saraswati to reach the love's lush valley,
build their love-nest there
with moonbeams and dream-rafters.

The Dance is Over
(*Kathaa Ta Sarichhi*)

Nothing is left
unsaid or undone,
the dance is over.
Let silence prevail
wishing well
to each other.

Uncanny things happen –
beads break loose
from their string's hold; strewn,
they exhibit a sadist's lust
for the stormy dark,
over the pristine moonshine.

My choking entrails
feel pulled out, exposed;
dreams melt away
to hide in desolate nights;
a pervading isolation
rules the roost.

Even rains visit
with lost enthusiasm,
the flames go out
without allowing the wind
to do its bit; I stand holding
the string, the kite shorn off.

Should we discuss
why the sun hots up,

or why our island
goes under watery grave?
Let me rather savor
my bitter silence.

Days pass by, a frigid time.
Is this calm the messenger
of an advancing storm?
Only the sleep's soporific retreat
doesn't bother me,
does not needle my conscience.

In fact, you being out of sight,
are out of my mind;
allow me my solitude,
as I have let you have yours;
let's be as good as
dead for each other.

The Boarder, Upstairs (*Ooparwaalaa*)

Total bedlam down here, o' Lord!
In desperation I shout aloud, shrill,
threatening to kill myself;
I throw wild tantrums. But he
remains unconcerned upstairs!

Exasperated, I threat to throw him out,
drown him, set fire to his assets. Curse him,

"Go to hell." But every such occasion, I
cajole him back, "How could you leave me,
my pet, packing away my heart?"

Is it so hard to accommodate me
into a normal home? My nature
an irritable itchy nettle bush?
I, a mad woman with a dirty mind,
you getting tired of me easily!

Like heavy rain on earth
we pound each other, each
tearing into the other, wallowing
in mutual mudslinging? Ours is a night,
we compete to make its darkness darker!

I know, it's a stormy patch
of life, I am perhaps going berserk.
But he, in his upper room, the unseen
director of all the drama, sits still
wearing a bemused silly smile!

Only For Your Sublime Presence (*Tame Achha Boli*)

Your sublime absence,
my seasons celebrate its mystique,
but I miss you, your quiet company,
a lotus missing its water world.

God, scriptures, and venerations
lose their significance;

I suffer from 'rift in the lute'
in walks of a solitary life.

Nightmares disappear from my sleep,
my cool is not encroached upon
by rage, lightness of the unbearable,
alluvium going arid without you.

Your muted presence creates an aura,
love doesn't ferment, but indifference at bay,
ordinary acts look gloriously tinted,
the dark wears a dazzle.

It gives me a surge of joy,
a school child's pleasure on hearing
the school's last bell; my love for you
does not singe, rather burnished by your fire.

The inert dolls
play in obedience for my joy,
the flowers appear to bloom
for my basket only.

Come back dear, step into my boudoir,
let us adorn the night with stars,
let our love, persistent and demanding,
bring smiles, not sighs of regret.

Black Eagle Books

www.blackeaglebooks.org
info@blackeaglebooks.org

Black Eagle Books, an independent publisher, was founded as a nonprofit organization in April, 2019. It is our mission to connect and engage the Indian diaspora and the world at large with the best of works of world literature published on a collaborative platform, with special emphasis on foregrounding Contemporary Classics and New Writing.

www.ingramcontent.com/pod-product-compliance
Lightning Source LLC
Chambersburg PA
CBHW020531080526
44583CB00013B/824